The New Archaeology and the Ancient Maya

THE NEW ARCHAEOLOGY AND THE ANCIENT MAYA

Jeremy A. Sabloff

SCIENTIFIC AMERICAN LIBRARY

A division of HPHLP
New York

Library of Congress Cataloging-in-Publication Data

Sabloff, Jeremy A.
    The new archaeology and the ancient Maya.

    Includes bibliographical references.
    1. Mayas—Antiquities.   2. Archaeology—Methodology.
3. Archaeology—Philosophy.   4. Mexico—Antiquities.
5. Central America—Antiquities.   I. Title.
F1435.S114   1990   972.81′016   89-10927
    ISBN 0-7167-5054-6 (W. H. Freeman)

ISSN 1040-3213

Printed in the United States of America.

Scientific American Library
A Division of HPHLP
New York

Distributed by W. H. Freeman and Company
41 Madison Avenue, New York, New York, 10010 and
20 Beaumont Street, Oxford OX1 2NQ, England

1 2 3 4 5 6 7 8 9 0   KP   8 9

This book is number 30 of a series.

To my in-laws
Berenice S. and M. William Weinberg
with affection

CONTENTS

It is the customary fate of new truths to begin as heresies and to end as superstitions.

—T. H. HUXLEY

When I began my career in Maya archaeology in the mid 1960s, I did not know I was walking into the middle of a revolution. Archaeologists were struggling to transform their discipline from an enterprise that produced impressionistic accounts and lists of dates into a science that tried to rigorously explain why cultures change. As the practice of archaeology has become more and more methodical over the past few decades, our understanding of many ancient civilizations has been transformed. I was lucky enough to participate in the creation of a new model of the ancient Maya civilization and decided to write the story of how changes in the practice of archaeology have reshaped our view of that civilization.

This book is not another addition to the already well-filled shelf of good introductions to the ancient Maya. Nor is the book a history of Maya studies. Rather, it is my attempt to explain how early archaeologists arrived at the "traditional model" of ancient Maya civilization that was popular in the first half of this century and how the new kinds of fieldwork and the recent intellectual shifts gave birth to a radically different view of the Maya. Through this story, I hope to convey an understanding of what archaeology can accomplish and how. In the natural course of my tale, readers should also gain a sense of lowland Maya civilization from before the time of Christ to the Spanish Conquest.

I owe the conception and completion of this volume to many people, only a few of whom I have the space to acknowledge. My mentors in Maya studies—Gordon Willey, Evon Vogt, and the late Ledyard and Robert Smith—helped ignite my interest in Maya archaeology and shaped my early thinking on the subject. Over the past twenty years at Harvard University, the University of Utah, the University of New Mexico, the University of Cambridge, and the University of Pittsburgh, I have been fortunate in sharing friendship and arguing ideas with a tremendously stimulating group of graduate students and colleagues. I also have shared the excitement of a rapidly changing discipline with a host of Maya archaeologists in the field, at meetings, and at lectures. I thank them all. I also thank Gair Tourtellot, my co-director on the Sayil Archaeological Project, with whom I have had many enlightening discussions about the ancient Maya for a number of years.

Great thanks are due to Jerry Lyons, who first proposed the idea for this book and who has continued to encourage me; Susan Moran, who vastly improved the style and flow of the text; Travis Amos, who

PREFACE

assiduously assembled the terrific photographs; Diane Maass, who carefully shepherded the book through production; Tomo Narashima, who drew the beautiful illustrations; Lynn Pieroni, who created the elegant design; and all their colleagues at the Scientific American Library. This has been my fourth opportunity to work with the superb professional staff at W. H. Freeman and, as with my past three books, it has been a great pleasure. I also gratefully acknowledge those many colleagues who supplied photographs for the book, whether used or not. I thank, too, Kelli Carmean, who prepared the Index.

Paula, Josh, and Lindi, as always, have been tremendously understanding during the writing of this volume. I dedicate the book with affection to my in-laws, Berenice S. Weinberg and M. William Weinberg, who have made life sweet for my family and have been so supportive all these years.

J. A. S.
Pittsburgh

July, 1989

The New Archaeology and the Ancient Maya

THE
GROWTH
OF
MODERN
SCIENTIFIC
ARCHAEOLOGY

The ruins of an ancient Maya building at Mayapán.

$\mathcal{I}$'m not particularly interested in ancient objects." This seemingly heretical statement for an archaeologist usually takes aback friends who believe that the best way to entertain me is to show me the local museum. On more than one occasion, I have had to explain that beautiful Classic Maya vases or finely carved jade pendants hold less interest to me—and to many of my colleagues—than the scientific investigation of ideas about why and how ancient cultures like the Maya developed. I do not have dreams of finding a fabulous burial chamber with hundreds of beautiful art objects, like a modern-day Howard Carter entering King Tut's tomb.

While I am impressed by those archaeologists who can look at a variety of objects and tell you their age, place of origin, and function, such activities are not the primary concern of many archaeologists, including myself. For us, the traditional "what," "where," and "when" questions of the archaeological enterprise are no longer ends in themselves, but have become means to answering the questions of "why" and "how." We want to understand what made an ancient people as they were, and we are eager to use all sorts of nontraditional methods to find out.

If you ask people on the street to picture an archaeologist, they are likely to describe a person digging in the middle of an excavation (probably dressed in khaki and wearing a pith helmet!) as dirt flies in all directions. But while contemporary archaeologists can often be found in the trenches, they are just as likely to be found seated at a computer terminal running multivariate analyses of distributions of artifacts found on a cave floor. Or they may be found hunched over binocular microscopes examining thin sections of prehistoric pottery sherds, or inspecting large satellite images for signs of early watercourses, or peering through high-tech, laser surveying instruments while mapping preindustrial urban centers. In attempts to link the material remains of a dead civilization with modern cultural activities, the graduate students who are studying with me are just as likely to be excavating in the house or yard of a modern Mexican peasant family as they are to be digging through an ancient Maya palace. Moreover, if you run into them on campus, they are as likely to be carrying a book on sampling strategies as on the Pre-Conquest Maya.

The practice of archaeology today is significantly different from that of just a few decades ago, not only in the battery of new hardware and sophisticated technical analyses now available, but in new approaches to interpreting the past and new methods of studying ancient

The romantic image of archaeology portrayed by the Indiana Jones movies and other films bears little resemblance to the reality of scientific archaeology today. Archaeologists actually spend countless hours in meticulous, often mundane research, such as the workers shown below collecting broken pieces of pots and flint at the ancient Maya site of Sayil. The aim is to understand the development of past culture, not to find lost arks.

UNITED STATES

MEXICO

Gulf of Mexico

Tula

Teotihuacán

Yucatán
Peninsula

BELIZE

HONDURAS

GUATEMALA

EL SALVADOR

Caribbean Sea

Pacific Ocean

The ancient Maya lived in an area encompassing modern-day Belize and Guatemala and parts of modern-day Mexico, Honduras, and El Salvador.

remains. These differences are the result of a series of intellectual upheavals in the discipline of archaeology since the early 1960s. The importance of these upheavals has been so far-reaching that some scholars describe them as having revolutionized the field.

In the past two decades, the transformation in archaeology, coupled with a vastly increased data base from recent research projects, has changed our understanding of many of the peoples of the ancient world. One dramatic example is the radical alteration in the archaeology of the ancient Maya, the vanished civilization that existed on and near the Yucatán Peninsula in Precolumbian times. In recent years, important new research has revolutionized interpretations of the growth of ancient Maya civilization. Because of the drastic revision in our understanding of the ancient Maya, as well as the familiarity of the general public with some of the great achievements of that culture, the archaeology of the Maya provides an ideal case study of the shifts that the discipline has undergone all over the world in the past few decades.

THE CHANGING NATURE OF ARCHAEOLOGICAL RESEARCH

Archaeologists, both traditional and modern, have always begun their work by examining the artifacts and debris left by ancient civilizations. The accumulated remains of past cultures are known as the archaeological record; they range from large buildings and monuments through skeletons, tools, and jewelry to tiny chips of stone or pottery. Relying on the archaeological record as their only physical evidence, archaeologists try to reconstruct the development of dead civilizations—to draw a picture of the daily lives of their people, and how those lives changed through time.

Until recently, archaeologists were concerned above all with deciphering the function of artifacts and placing them in time and space. Suppose that an archaeologist was interested in a ceramic vessel. He or she would first ask, *What* is this ceramic vessel? What did the ancient people use it for? After careful reasoning, the archaeologist might decide it was a cooking pot. In this most fundamental yet treacherous task of archaeology, the archaeologist has taken a meaningless piece of material and given it a significance and purpose. He or she has taken the first step in interpreting a culture.

Traditional archaeologists would go on to ask, *Where* was the pot manufactured and *when*? If they were studying the ancient Maya, for example, the answer might be, along a stretch of the Pasión River in Guatemala between A.D. 300 and 600. After examining and reaching conclusions about a large number of artifacts, archaeologists would be in a position to tackle larger issues, such as, When and where did the Classic Maya civilization arise? Whether speaking of the simplest implement or an entire civilization, traditional archaeologists would still couch most questions in terms of "what," "where," and "when."

Modern archaeologists still ask these questions, but they don't stop there—the goals of archaeology today are far more ambitious. Beginning in the early 1960s, certain archaeologists, foremost among them Lewis R. Binford of the University of New Mexico, argued that archaeology should adopt the goal traditionally held by anthropologists of explaining the process of cultural change over long periods of time. Although lip service had been paid to anthropological goals prior to the early 1960s, little had been done to advance these ends, and theories of why cultures changed were either ignored or derided as speculation. Rather than focusing their attention just on the

The Classic Maya artists produced beautifully painted ceramic vessels such as this vase from Copán. It depicts a seated ruler wearing an elaborate headdress and other ornamentation including nose and ear plugs. A hieroglyphic inscription circles the vase just below the rim.

traditional "what," "where," and "when" questions that had dominated archaeological practice, scholars today agree on the need to zero in on the "why" and "how" questions of culture process. The shift in goals has been perhaps the most significant change giving rise to the "new" archaeology.

For Maya archaeologists, the recent attention to culture process means that instead of concentrating solely on particular artifacts and their place in time and space, they are now also investigating how Maya civilization flowered. Did it develop because of growing internal complexity or because of influences from more advanced neighbors? Did growing population cause internal conflicts, which in turn led to the more complex political organization needed to raise armies and build defensive structures? Or, on the other hand, did increasing political complexity come about because expanding long-distance trade required more sophisticated means of handling exchanges, production, and distribution?

Maya archaeologists excavating a site in the tropical lowlands of the Yucatán Peninsula might find pieces of obsidian, a volcanic glass, in their trenches. In the past, they would have compared these artifacts with similar ones from other sites and inferred that their bladelike form with its sharp edges indicated that the artifacts probably were used for cutting. They also would have pointed out that the lack of volcanoes in the lowlands meant that the obsidian must have been traded into the site from the adjacent volcanic highlands.

Maya archaeologists today would go much further in their analyses. Using new chemical techniques, archaeologists can pinpoint exactly from where in the highlands the obsidian pieces derive. Depending on the specific research questions they are pursuing, they might carefully sift and screen the excavated earth in search of chipping debris that would reveal if finished tools were being traded or if the tools were being manufactured on site. They might examine the area of the discovery to see if the obsidian tools are found in domestic settings, and, if so, whether they are found only in elite residences or in peasant ones as well. They might measure the widths and lengths of the blades and compare them with ones from other lowland sites to see if the size of the blades changes with the distance from the highland source. They also might try to find out if these sizes changed over the years. These and other analyses might then be used to test different hypotheses about where the trade routes began and where they went, how they were controlled, and whether they changed through time. All such research would be part of more general strategies aimed at understanding the nature of Maya civilization—in these cases, its economic or political aspects—and how and why it evolved over the centuries of its development.

As the new archaeology began questioning what factors were involved in the growth of cultural complexity, interest also grew in the role of the environment. The older "possibilism" had held the environment more or less constant in archaeological thinking—the environment was seen as "background" or the "setting" for cultural development. This view was replaced by a modified determinism that recognized the environment as a factor in cultural change.

To successfully broach "why" and "how" questions, the new archaeologists maintained that new views of culture were necessary. The traditional or normative view, which was derived from the perspective that dominated American cultural anthropology for most of this century, emphasized shared ideas. According to this view, all members of a culture shared an ideal mental template that they were taught as

The ancient city of Tikal was the largest and most impressive of the great Maya centers. After centuries of prosperity, Tikal, along with many other cities in the Southern Maya Lowlands, fell into rapid decline. One of the key questions of Maya archaeology is, Why did Tikal and other Classic centers collapse?

children. These shared ideas were expressed in cultural traits, and cultures were characterized by long lists of these traits. Such traits included the way pottery was made and decorated, the method for building houses, or the nature of the spiritual world and the deities populating it. The overall emphasis was on the homogeneity of cultures.

The new archaeologists argued that the normative view ignored or deemphasized the variability of culture. Moreover, its stress on ideas and mental templates made it difficult for archaeologists to employ. The new archaeologists championed a systems view of culture, which has rapidly won wide adoption among scholars. Following a minority strain of thought in cultural anthropology, they viewed culture as a system with different subsystems having changing adaptive roles through time. The technological subsystem, for example, would consist of the workers, tools, materials, and techniques linked with exploitation of the environment, while economic and political subsystems would be in charge of organizing such exploitation. The new archaeologists contended that one of the archaeologist's tasks was to correlate material remains with different cultural subsystems. Once archaeologists had identified different subsystems, they could attempt to understand how these subsystems were linked together. The advocates of a systems view maintained that instead of sharing culture, people participated in culture, and that they participated differently.

The adoption of a systems perspective of culture had immediate implications for archaeological methodology, because if cultures are not generally homogeneous, then the question of sampling becomes critical. Since it is usually not possible to study an entire site in detail, archaeologists perforce must examine only parts of sites—sometimes only small parts. If culture is conceived as being homogenous, it is not a critical matter where one excavates, because excavations anywhere at the site should produce similar materials. However, if archaeologists want to understand variability, then they must employ sampling strategies that will give them confidence that their sample is representative of the whole site.

If archaeologists plan to excavate a limited number of houses, for instance, they need to devise a sampling procedure that assures them that they are not missing out on an important class of house. On a finer scale, they cannot simply dig a pit in the middle of the remains of a house, but need to sample the interior and exterior of the house, as well as seemingly vacant areas adjacent. Fortunately, with the aid of

computers, archaeologists today can use a variety of statistical techniques to grapple with the problems of sampling. Furthermore, such techniques help archaeologists recognize meaningful patterns in a confusing jumble of data. Analyses of this kind might reveal, for example, that small flint chips are consistently found off the back end of platforms supporting residential structures. After follow-up excavations, archaeologists might be able to infer that family workshops were located off-platform and that certain flint tools used in domestic activities were manufactured there. Excavations made solely within rooms or just on top of platforms would miss such potentially important patterns.

The new archaeologists defended all of these new initiatives as making procedures in the discipline more "scientific." In effect, they were arguing that the field had reached a dead end because it lacked rigorous methodologies—that is, useful, systematic research procedures. By the 1960s, field and laboratory techniques for obtaining data had become quite sophisticated and highly productive—archaeologists were now able to measure the age and composition of a wide range of artifacts and reconstruct changing environments in great detail. Yet some means was needed to combine these techniques

This simple rubble platform may have supported a hut made of wood and thatch. In this case, archaeologists have excavated the lower right corner of the platform. To ensure proper sampling of potential variability, they must study a number of examples and either excavate entire platforms and their immediate surrounding areas or excavate different sections of other platforms.

within a systematic set of procedures designed to answer specific questions. Researchers had to set out to solve clearly stated problems and then design a methodology for each problem. For example, if an archaeologist was interested in understanding how ancient peoples adapted to an environment, then he or she would need to employ a methodology that would show how peoples distributed themselves over the landscape and whether there were correlations between certain features of the landscape and features of the settlement. Sound methodologies would permit scholars to validate hypotheses unambiguously; no longer would an idea be judged according to the prestige of its proponents.

By the 1970s, it became clear to some scholars, such as Michael Schiffer of the University of Arizona and Lewis Binford, that one of the key methodological issues is how to link cultural activities of the past with the archaeological record of the present. What can piles of broken pottery or faded murals tell us about how a people lived? Two kinds of issues are involved here. One is the whole question of how the archaeological record—the remains on and beneath the ground that scholars view at the present moment—is formed and what transformations it undergoes between its original formation and the modern day. The archaeological record of today is not a direct reflection of ancient activities—the material remains of a past civilization have been altered both by natural processes such as the decay over time of wooden walls and thatched roofs and by cultural processes such as reuse by a later culture. Archaeologists may not find any cut stone around ancient Maya houses because modern peasants have removed these stones to use for walls or road bedding, or recent plowing might have destroyed some remains and rearranged others. Sites along river banks might become covered with alluvium that buries formerly visible artifacts. Surveys that do not dig below the surface might arrive at totally inaccurate conclusions about how ancient peoples exploited the river shore. Therefore, archaeologists must understand the kinds of transformations that the record might undergo from the time artifacts are discarded or a site is abandoned.

The second issue is how to link the present record with past behaviors in as unambiguous a fashion as possible. Archaeologists now believe that the archaeological record has no inherent meaning. A particular feature of the archaeological record, for instance, does not mean "house." Rather, the archaeologist of today sees a rectangular alignment of rocks and begins to look for clues as to what these rocks could have been. Finding that modern peasant houses have wooden walls and a single row of stones as a foundation, the archaeologist might infer based on analogy that the pattern of rocks is the remains of an ancient house built many centuries ago of mostly perishable materials. In other words, the modern archaeological record cannot "speak" to archaeologists as informants speak to ethnographers. Rather, archaeologists imbue the record with meaning. How they do this is the critical issue.

When traditional archaeologists had spotted a repeated feature of the archaeological record, they would usually assign a particular meaning to that feature by making an informal inference. For example, Maya archaeologists inferred that bounded open spaces in ceremonial centers were marketplaces. The inference was arrived at through analogy to modern Maya communities where markets are held in large plazas. This procedure had a fatal flaw: the inference was not investigated further, and after a while it became an assumption. What originally had been a tentative statement of the form "because x (a feature of the archaeological record) shares certain characterisitics with y (a known feature of the present), then other aspects of y can be

Did the ancient Maya have markets similar to this modern Maya market in the Guatemala highlands? Possibly, but archaeologists will know only after comparing the leftover debris of modern markets with patterns in the archaeological record.

inferred for x" turned into a given. In other words, a potential meaning derived from a tentative analogy became over time a stipulated "fact" of the record. More general inferences, such as "historic and modern Maya agriculturalists practiced slash-and-burn agriculture, therefore the ancient Maya did, too," also, through time, were accepted as facts. But, as we shall see in the next chapter, such "facts" are not facts at all since the inferences they were based on now appear to be unwarranted. When two archaeologists "saw" different "facts"—that is, recognized similar patterns in the archaeological record and offered different analogies to assign meaning—more often than not the scholar offering the interpretation would be judged rather than the rigor of his or her analogy.

Most archaeologists now recognize such procedures as unproductive and therefore unacceptable. Archaeologists today are searching for much more rigorous means to bridge the archaeological record and past activities—in particular, stronger and better analogies that attempt to link the static record with dynamic behavior. These analogies are no longer assumed to be true, but are subject to testing and validation.

In the search for stronger analogies, archaeologists are undertaking their own studies, often called ethnoarchaeology, of the material behavior of modern peoples. Here, a team under the supervision of the archaeologist Michael Smyth excavates a hut used by modern Maya for storage. They hope that any physical remains they find will help archaeologists interpret the remains of ancient Maya storage facilities.

Finally, along with clear goals, new perspectives on culture, modern field and laboratory techniques, and more rigorous methods, the new archaeologists have brought to the discipline a new optimism. Archaeology had long been regarded as a second-class citizen in the house of anthropology, able to explore only limited parts of the material world or peoples of the past because of the supposed inferiority of the archaeological data base. Time destroys many aspects of material culture, and in societies without written records, nonmaterial features of culture such as kinship terms or religious observances cannot be observed. The new archaeologists contended that with stronger, more explicit methods, they would be bound not by the limitations of the archaeological record but by the limitations of inferences. And, as inferences became better, so would the possibilities of testing hypotheses about how and why cultures develop over long periods of time. Although the data and methodologies archaeologists work with are different from those of ethnologists or cultural anthropologists who study the cultures of modern peoples, archaeologists potentially have just as good an opportunity to learn about the nature of culture change as their ethnological colleagues. In fact, with their long time perspective, archaeologists might even have some advantages over ethnologists, whose time scales are usually measured in months or years, not centuries or millennia.

In sum, archaeologists are now attempting to employ much more rigorous or "scientific" research procedures. Assumptions are being made explicit, research strategies are carefully delineated, and hypotheses are put forward in testable form. With such a methodological framework in place, older, intuitively based understandings are being challenged and either strengthened or replaced.

THE ANCIENT MAYA AS A CASE STUDY

"Tall temple-pyramids towering above a jungle canopy." "Long, multiroomed palaces looming over broad, open plazas." "Intricately carved stone monuments with stern-visaged, elaborately garbed figures surrounded by complex hieroglyphic inscriptions." These romantic visions might well come into the minds of knowledgeable readers and even professional archaeologists when the words "ancient Maya" are uttered. Thus, it should come as no surprise that the early intensive field research on the Maya, from the late nineteenth century to the

The impressive monumental architecture at the heart of the great site of Tikal towers above its jungle setting.

Facing page: The cities of the ancient Maya world were spread throughout the highlands and lowlands.

middle of this century, concentrated on such obvious traits as temples and palaces and on the materials in tombs and caches found with the great architecture and the carved monuments.

The romantic image of the Maya was encouraged by their exotic location and distance in time. The heartland of Maya civilization lies in the lowlands of the modern countries of Mexico, Guatemala, Belize, and Honduras. The lowlands are situated in the vast Yucatán Peninsula and the immediate surrounding area, and they cover approximately 390,000 square kilometers. Dense tropical rainforest or jungle cover most of the Southern Lowlands, while the Northern Lowlands are dominated by scrub forest. The distinct rainy season yields a high annual rainfall, with up to 400 centimeters falling each year in parts of the Southern Lowlands. Although rivers such as the Usumacinta on the western frontier of the lowlands and the New and Hondo in Belize played important roles in moving goods and peoples, much of the Maya realm is landlocked and must have seemed remote and inaccessible to most Westerners.

Another group of Maya lived in the vastly different environment of the highlands. This upland area is centered in modern Guatemala

Isla Cerritos

Komchén
Dzibilchaltún
Izamal
Chichén Itzá
Cobá
Oxkintok
Mayapán
Xelhá
San Gervasio
Uxmal
Kabáh
Tancah
Sayil
Labná
Tulum
Island of Cozumel

GULF OF MEXICO

NORTHERN
LOWLANDS

Edzná

QUINTANA ROO

CAMPECHE

Becán
Rio Bec
Hondo River
Cerros
Nohmul
Pulltrouser
Cuello
Swamp
Xicalango
Candelaria River
Lamanai
TABASCO
Usumacinta River
El Mirador
San José
New River
Belize River
Palenque
Uaxactún
Holmul
SOUTHERN
Tikal
Barton Ramie
LOWLANDS
Yaxchilán
Bonampak
Seibal
Altar de Sacrificios
Pasión River
CHIAPAS
Dos Pilas

NORTHERN HIGHLANDS
Lake Izabal
Quiriguá
Naco
Izapa
Copán
Kaminaljuyú
SOUTHERN HIGHLANDS

The rugged mountains of the Maya highlands are a strong contrast to the jungles of the lowlands.

but stretches from the Chiapas highlands of Mexico in the north to the mountains of El Salvador in the south. Rugged volcanic peaks and high ranges separate valleys of differing size. The Maya of this upland area spoke languages related to those of the lowland Maya, but formed distinct cultural groupings.

The Maya had settled in the lowlands by 800 B.C., if not earlier, and flourished in various lowland regions until the Spanish Conquest in the sixteenth century A.D. Millions of Maya-speaking peoples thrive today in both the lowlands and highlands. Yet although some Maya traditions survived the Conquest, their modern culture is vastly different from that of Prehispanic times. In effect, the Conquest destroyed Maya civilization, and the Maya had to adapt to a radically altered cultural world.

Archaeologists traditionally have divided ancient Maya history into the three principal periods shown in the chart on the following page: the Preclassic (800 B.C. to A.D. 300), the Classic (A.D. 300 to 900), and the Postclassic (A.D. 900 to 1520). Each of these periods had distinct styles of ceramics and architecture. The Classic period, with its beautifully built temples and palaces, its intricately carved stelae with hieroglyphic inscriptions, and its elaborate polychrome pots, has been traditionally seen as the height of Maya civilization. The relatively modest agricultural villages of the Preclassic period lacked these impressive achievements, while the Postclassic period was a time of decline in the high artistic and architectural skills that had flourished during the Classic.

The early archaeologists focused on the impressive Classic monuments of Maya civilization; in so doing, they were emphasizing that civilization's elite features—those aspects of culture having to do with upper-class priests and rulers. This preoccupation with the upper class was very much in keeping with the mainstream of archaeological research in the Americas and was further fueled by the demands of museums for fine display materials—the products of elite culture. In the decades around World War II, the results of continuing field research were crystallized in a model of how Maya civilization functioned—a model that emphasized elite accomplishments. This model, particularly as expounded by the great Maya archaeologist J. Eric S. Thompson in his popular writings, gained widespread acceptance and has had much influence on archaeologists' thinking about the Maya until very recently. It is a view that tourists to Maya sites are still apt to hear from guides and read in the popular literature.

In the past three decades, however, new research has shown that many of the tenets of this "traditional model" are incorrect. In part, its mistaken views were the result of the relatively limited field data available until recently. But new data were not the only factor undermining the prevailing model of Maya civilization. New techniques, in both the

Conquest

1500•

Late Postclassic

1400•

1300•

1200•

Early Postclassic

1100•

1000•

900•   (Terminal Classic)

800•

700•

600•

Classic

500•

400•

300•

200•

100•

A.D.
B.C.

Late Preclassic

100•

200•

300•

400•

500•

Middle Preclassic

600•

700•

800•

900•

field and the laboratory, and innovative methodologies also made available new *kinds* of information. In addition, the wide-scale attempts to make archaeological procedures more rigorous encouraged archaeologists to reinterpret existing data and threw light on evidence that had been ignored. As a result of this work, a broader, more encompassing model of Maya civilization has recently emerged in the archaeological literature. In the pages that follow, I will examine first the traditional model of Maya civilization and then the new model, showing how shifts in the science of archaeology have transformed our interpretation of lowland Maya civilization.

Facing page: The principal chronological periods of Precolumbian Maya history. Typical styles of architecture from each period are represented by the temples at the right: the Late Preclassic temple-pyramid at Uaxactún (Structure E-VIIsub), with stucco masks flanking its stairways; the soaring Classic Temple I at Tikal; and the heavily stuccoed, colonnaded Late Postclassic Temple of the Frescoes at Tulum.

THE
TRADITIONAL
MODEL
OF
ANCIENT
MAYA
CIVILIZATION

Elaborately clothed stucco figures on the wall
of Pacal's crypt at Palenque

Found in Palenque in the Southern Lowlands, this rubbing from a stone slab shows a hieroglyphic inscription that had been carved in low relief.

According to conventional wisdom, Maya civilization rose around A.D. 300 in the Southern Lowlands and flourished for more than five hundred years at a number of major sites such as Tikal, Copán, and Palenque. Understanding of the great achievements of Maya civilization was built up from the late nineteenth century to the mid-twentieth century through the brilliant, path-breaking research of a number of scholars who braved difficult field conditions to study the remains of the ancient Maya. Among the most articulate and influential of this pioneering group were the Englishman Sir J. Eric S. Thompson and the American Sylvanus G. Morley, who were two of the foremost exponents and popularizers of the "establishment" views of ancient Maya civilization.

Thompson, Morley, and their colleagues were profoundly impressed by the tremendous intellectual and artistic accomplishments of the Maya. They documented and studied the monumental feats of the Maya, particularly the huge stone temples and palaces they found by the hundreds throughout the Yucatán Peninsula. They recorded and analyzed innumerable hieroglyphic texts discovered on carved stelae, or large stone slabs. Through time they built up a deep and abiding love and respect for all things Maya. They felt that the deeds of the Maya in their exotic jungle setting were unique and unrivaled.

Thompson and Morley were especially successful in synthesizing the results of both their own researches and those of their compatriots. Their written surveys articulated the dominant views of the development of Maya civilization and formed the basis of what I will call the traditional model of the ancient Maya in the pages that follow.

THE CONVENTIONAL VIEW OF THE ANCIENT MAYA

According to the traditional model, the period from A.D. 300 to 900, known as the Classic period, was the height of Maya civilization. Until lately the bulk of archaeological attention focused on this period and on the southern or tropical rainforest portion of the Yucatán Peninsula known as the Southern Lowlands.

The traditional view of the Maya was a romantic and impressionistic one based on limited archaeological data from the centers of large sites. Among its major assumptions, perhaps the most important was that the Classic Maya were not an urban society. Their civilization

was focused on a series of "vacant" centers where only priests, rulers, and their acolytes lived. The bulk of the population were peasant farmers scattered in surrounding rural areas. Regular markets and important religious festivals brought people into the centers for short visits only. Although Maya scholars called these centers "cities," they clearly had a special definition in mind. As Eric Thompson noted, the Maya city "was not at all a city in our sense of the word, because it was a ceremonial, not an urban, center."

It was held that the great achievements of the Maya elite in their ceremonial centers were made possible through the support of nearby rural farmers. The surrounding populace built the huge structures that were the most visible aspect of the centers, and the farmers supplied the rulers with food. In return the priests interceded with the gods on behalf of the people to ensure adequate rains, good harvests, and the survival of the community.

Traditional archaeologists assumed that the peasants, like the modern Maya in Mexico and Guatemala today, practiced a kind of farming known as slash-and-burn or swidden agriculture. In this system, the peasants laboriously cleared fields in the forest or jungle with

As drawn by archaeologist Tatiana Pros-kouriakoff, this reconstruction of Copán at its height during the Late Classic period is an excellent example of the traditional view of Maya cities as non-urban centers. Few structures are depicted outside of the ceremonial core, except for an occasional thatched hut such as that in the lower right-hand corner.

Farmers practicing slash-and-burn agriculture carry out the following steps in sequence, shown from left to right above: (1) clearing a plot, (2) letting the vegetation dry, (3) burning the plot, (4) planting for a couple of years, and (5) letting the plot go fallow for at least eight years. Once the soil has recovered, the plot can be cleared again, and the cycle continues.

stone axes, leaving the dead trees and undergrowth to dry until they could be burned. Seeds would be planted in the burned fields just prior to the rainy season. The fields could be planted and harvested for two years before they were allowed to lie fallow for eight or ten years. The poor soils needed years of rest in order to replenish the nutrients that were rapidly lost while the field was under cultivation and open to the sun. Meanwhile, new fields would be cleared and burned. Because only a relatively small percentage of land could be under cultivation at any one time, the peasants needed a large territory to grow enough to feed themselves and the priestly elite. Archaeologists attributed the lack of urban development directly to the centrifugal force of the shifting agricultural practices.

Like their historic and modern descendants, the ancient Maya planted the "great triumvirate" of New World crops: maize (corn), beans, and squash. Together, these vegetables supplied most of the essential nutrients the Maya needed to survive.

It was conventionally argued that the priests spent the bulk of their time in esoteric pursuits, such as studying the skies and interpreting portents (what we would call today astrology and divination). They and their acolyte/scribes wrote down the results of their astronomical observations and calculations on folded screens made of bark paper. They also painted hieroglyphic inscriptions on murals and beautiful polychrome vases and carved inscriptions on stone monu-

ments. The inscriptions referred to calendrics, astronomy, and ab-
struse religious concerns related to the passage of time. According to
the prevailing canon, the Maya did not record historical events or
economic transactions, as the ancient Egyptians, Sumerians, and Babylonians did.

The relationship between the priests and the secular rulers was
ambiguous. Some scholars saw the two as one and the same, while
others viewed them as separate but equal or nearly equal in power and
authority. Whatever the exact situation, political rule was seen as the-
ocratic.

Above all, the traditional model portrayed the Maya as peaceful.
The politically independent ceremonial centers lived in harmony with
one another, each controlling its own hinterlands. Tikal, Copán, and
the other great Maya centers were portrayed as less contentious, New
World examples of Athens, Sparta, and the well-known city-states of
ancient Greece.

According to the prevailing perspective, the Maya in their jungle
lowland setting were relatively isolated from their neighbors. The
Maya were one of a group of advanced cultures in the area called
"Mesoamerica" stretching from northern Mexico south to what is now
Honduras and El Salvador. Yet traditional archaeologists thought that
all during Classic times, the Maya were shielded by their location and
environment from the ebb and flow of political and economic develop-

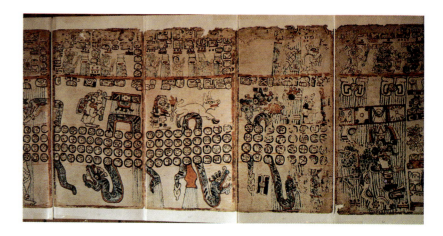

Only four Maya books, or codices, from before the Conquest have survived. The lost
codices were destroyed by the Spanish, or else
the fragile bark paper disintegrated naturally.
The codex shown here is the so-called Madrid
Codex, which is preserved in Spain.

ments elsewhere in ancient Mexico, particularly in the highlands of
Central Mexico and the Valley of Oaxaca, where the great cities of
Teotihuacán and Monte Alban reached their heights. In part, the
Maya were protected by distance (over 1,000 kilometers to the Valley
of Mexico and over 700 kilometers to Oaxaca) and in part by the
rugged terrain that separated the lowlands from the highlands. Therefore, it was believed that in the midst of change elsewhere in Mesoamerica, they remained unaffected by the militarism and materialism of
the "less cultured" and more worldly Central Mexicans. There may
have been an unconscious circularity in this contention. The isolation
of the Maya allowed them to maintain what was seen as a relatively
homogeneous culture, while their homogeneous culture helped them
resist potential changes introduced from outside the lowlands.

As just noted, traditional archaeologists believed that the behavior and customs of the ancient Maya were essentially the same from
one end of the lowlands to the other throughout the Classic period. For
instance, their centers were laid out in similar ways, they had the
identical writing system, their deities were duplicated from place to
place, their ceramics were alike, as were their stone tools, and their
buildings were duplicated over the entire area. Some differences in
style were recognized; for example, Copán artists carved monuments
in the round, while others used two-dimensional flat slabs. Yet these
differences were seen as insignificant compared to the broad similarities in Maya culture from site to site. Moreover, although changes

occurred between A.D. 300 and 900, they were thought to be relatively minor compared with the overall continuity of the period.

Around A.D. 800, the Southern Lowland cities went into a decline, and Classic civilization collapsed within a century. There was much argument about the causes of the collapse, with agricultural failure and peasant revolt two of the favored hypotheses. As the Southern Lowlands were virtually abandoned, the Northern Lowlands became more prominent, although archaeologists disagreed about the dating of developments in the Northern Lowlands at this time. One group saw the major Puuc region sites in the hilly portion of the western side of the Northern Lowlands—including Uxmal, Kabah, Sayil, and Labná—reaching their climax toward the end of the Classic period and collapsing at roughly the same time as the centers in the south. According to Eric Thompson and other champions of this view, the Postclassic period was ushered in when the Toltecs of Central Mexico invaded the Northern Lowlands in the tenth century and conquered Chichén Itzá. That city in turn flourished for a few centuries and controlled much of the north before it too collapsed. Its place was taken by the city of Mayapán, which ruled a confederation of provinces in northern Yucatán from the thirteenth century until the mid-

The stone maize god from Copán (right) is sculpted in a fully three-dimensional style, while the jade maize god from Palenque (left) is a two-dimensional bas-relief. Despite the difference in styles between these two distant sites, the features of the maize gods are remarkably similar, demonstrating that communication was widespread among the ancient Maya.

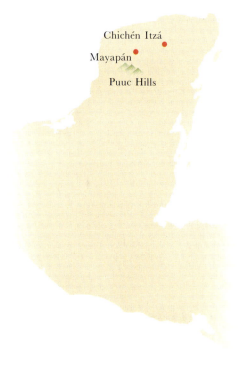

Chichén Itzá

Mayapán

Puuc Hills

fifteenth century. By the time the Spanish arrived less than a hundred years later, the Maya realm consisted of a number of independent centers with no central leadership.

An alternate view was supported by the great Mayanist Sylvanus Morley, who directed the major archaeological project at Chichén Itzá. According to Morley, the Puuc centers did not begin to flourish until after the collapse of Maya civilization in the south. This "resurgence" in the north marked the beginning of the Postclassic period, or the "New Empire." It was the result of a population movement from the south to the north and the migration of Mexicans or Mexican-influenced peoples into the Northern Lowlands. These people took over Chichén Itzá in A.D. 987 and founded the Puuc centers at about the same time. Chichén Itzá and the Puuc sites survived until around A.D. 1200, when they were abandoned and Mayapán rose to prominence.

To Eric Thompson and others, the start of the Postclassic period marked the beginning of the end of Maya civilization. Not only had the Classic centers collapsed in the Southern Lowlands, but Maya civilization as a whole had begun a long decline from its former heights, which lasted until the Spanish Conquest brought an end to it in the sixteenth century. The introduction of foreign Mexican culture traits, as well as "an internal dry rot in Maya culture," led to the "decadence" of Maya civilization. The carving of hieroglyphic inscriptions virtually ceased, architecture became smaller and shoddier, and the high art style became relatively impoverished. By the rise of Mayapán in the Late Postclassic or Decadent period (A.D. 1250–1520), Maya culture had seriously deteriorated from the glory days of the Classic period. The archaeologist Harry Pollock states, "It is quite clear that Mayapán fell heir to an impoverished culture. Over its life the city was subjected to numerous outside influences, but instead of finding a stimulus in them the result was a sterile eclecticism, a culture without vitality." Pollock further notes that "the age was materialistic," while Thompson sums up his feelings when he says, "The degeneration in all the arts in this last period of Maya history is really heartbreaking. I feel it is a manifestation of great cultural dislocation resulting from a shift from a hierarchic to a secular and militaristic culture." With the fall of Mayapán in the mid-fifteenth century, the Maya suffered political fragmentation as well—although perhaps no worse than in the Classic Southern Lowlands many centuries before. Nevertheless, according to Thompson, the Maya found by the Spanish in the early sixteenth century were a far cry from the magnificent culture of the eighth century.

In sum, Thompson, Morley, and their colleagues viewed the ancient Maya as unique, not only in the specifics of their culture, but in their general course of development in Classic times. Their civilization, it was declared, was different from other civilizations in Mexico and elsewhere in the ancient world not in degree but in kind. Their special, isolated rainforest setting produced a peaceful, harmonious

The Temple of the Diving God at Tulum is a good example of what archaeologists traditionally thought of as "decadent" in Late Postclassic architecture. Heavy coats of plaster originally covered the poorly cut and prepared stonework.

environment that permitted the unparalleled intellectual and artistic accomplishments of the Maya that we can still wonder at and admire today. This image of the Maya was persuasively argued by the leaders in the field and generally accepted by both scholars and amateur enthusiasts alike.

Morley's influential general text on *The Ancient Maya* appeared in 1946, while Thompson's equally important work *The Rise and Fall of Maya Civilization* came out in 1954. By the time Morley and Thompson came to write these books, they had each had long exposure—more than three decades for Morley and nearly three decades for Thompson—to both the remains of Maya civilization and the culture of the modern Maya. As might be expected, these experiences strongly colored their interpretations of the extant data on the ancient Maya. But what was the nature of the data that Morley and Thompson elucidated in their model of ancient Maya civilization and how were the data collected? Let us turn to the century or so of research that provided the foundation for the accepted wisdom propounded by Morley and Thompson.

EARLY EXPLORATIONS

The beginnings of Maya archaeology can be marked by the joint explorations in 1839 and 1841 of the American lawyer/diplomat John Stephens and the English architect/artist Frederick Catherwood, recorded in their subsequent publications *Incidents of Travel in Central America, Chiapas, and Yucatán* (1841) and *Incidents of Travel in Yucatán* (1843). Fresh from his travels in Egypt and the Mediterranean and his best-selling books *Incidents of Travel in Egypt, Arabia Petraea and the Holy Land* and *Incidents of Travel in Greece, Turkey, Russia and Poland*, Stephens hit just the right note with a public readership that was intensely curious about the ancient civilizations of Mexico and Central America. His descriptions of the Maya ruins were careful, rich in detail, and free of the rampant speculations that were characteristic of the age. Catherwood's drawings, too, were descriptive rather than imaginative, and relatively accurate for the time.

Stephens' discussion of the interior of the quadrangle he calls the House of the Nuns at the site of Uxmal in the Puuc region of northern Yucatán is a good example of his descriptive style:

Passing through the arched gateway, we enter a noble courtyard, with four great facades looking down upon it, each ornamented from one end to the other with the richest and most intricate carving known in the art of the builders of Uxmal; presenting a scene of strange magnificence, surpassing any that is now to be seen among its ruins. This courtyard is two hundred and fourteen feet wide, and two hundred and fifty-eight feet deep. At the time of our first entrance it was overgrown with bushes and grass, quails started up from underneath our feet, and, with a whirring flight, passed over the tops of the buildings. Whenever we went to it, we started flocks of these birds, and throughout the whole of our residence at Uxmal they were the only disturbers of its silence and desolation.

Stephens and Catherwood romantically emphasized the mysterious nature of ancient Maya civilization and focused on the biggest and most visible of the standing buildings and monuments. Stephens described his party's entrance into the great site of Copán on the southeast frontier of the lowland Maya realm as follows:

The popular appeal of Stephens' travelogues was enhanced by Frederick Catherwood's drawings, including this detail from a facade on the western side of the House of the Nuns at Uxmal.

31

The splendid artistic acheivements of the ancient Maya were brought to the eye of the general public through Catherwood's careful renderings of monuments such as the Copán stela illustrated here. The stela depicts a ruler of Copán in full regalia.

The wall was of cut stone, well laid, and in a good state of preservation. We ascended by large stone steps, in some places perfect, and in others thrown down by trees which had grown up between the crevices, and reached a terrace, the form of which it was impossible to make out, from the density of forest in which it was enveloped. Our guide cleared a way with his machete, and we passed, as it lay half buried in the earth, a large fragment of stone elaborately sculptured, and came to the angle of a structure with steps on the sides, in form and appearance, so far as the trees would enable us to make it out, like the sides of a pyramid. Diverging from the base, and working our way through the thick woods, we came upon a square stone column, about fourteen feet high and three feet on each side, sculptured in very bold relief, and on all four of the sides, from the base to the top. The front was the figure of a man curiously and richly dressed, and the face, evidently a portrait, solemn, stern, and well fitted to excite terror. The back was of a different design, unlike anything we had ever seen before, and the sides were covered with hieroglyphics. This our guide called an "Idol;" and before it, at a distance of three feet, was a large block of stone, also sculptured with figures and emblematic devices, which he called an altar. The sight of this unexpected monument put at rest at once and forever, in our minds, all uncertainty in regard to the character of American antiquities, and gave us the assurance that the objects we were in search of were interesting, not only as the remains of an unknown people, but as works of art, proving, like newly discovered historical records, that the people who once occupied the Continent of America were not savages.

The juxtaposition of the difficult and alien—at least to readers in North America and Europe—environment with the beauty of the great architectural structures became a theme that was to dominate not only the age of nineteenth-century exploration but much of the professional archaeology of this century.

Although earlier explorers had begun to fill in the lowland map with descriptions of Maya sites, Stephens and Catherwood made a major leap in this regard. Their pioneering work was followed up throughout the nineteenth century by a number of other explorers, including Desiré Charnay, Alice and Augustus Le Plongeon, Edward H. Thompson, and Teobert Maler, who not only found new sites but described more fully previously reported ones. Again, virtually all their attention was directed to the reporting of large stone temples and palaces and carved stone monuments.

Of all these individuals perhaps the most significant for the development of Maya archaeology was the Englishman Alfred P.

Maudslay. As the Maya scholar Harry Pollock has put it, "The first archaeologist in the Maya field that may be called modern was Alfred Maudslay. His extensive explorations, combined with some excavation, resulted in a large body of illustrative material possessing of accuracy and excellence previously unknown." For thirteen years beginning in 1881, Maudslay made plans of a limited number of sites in greater detail than had been done in the past and photographed and drew the major structures and stone carvings at these sites. He had sufficient confidence in the accuracy of his drawings to publish them side by side with his photographs. Maudslay published the results of his research in eight volumes (four of text and four of illustrations) of the huge multivolume *Biologia Centrali-Americana*.

Maudslay was particularly concerned with recording the numerous hieroglyphic inscriptions, which were most often found on carved limestone stelae. The inscriptions contained series of symbolic characters, or glyphs, that could be completely abstract in form or could be quite realistic figures. The nineteenth-century explorers recognized

Left: This shot of the tower at Palenque in 1889 is one of the superb photographs published by Maudslay. *Right:* Alfred P. Maudslay at his field "office" inside a vaulted room at Palenque.

1,212

The number 1,212 expressed in the Maya arithmetical system.

the hieroglyphs as writing, first through information gleaned from discussions of Maya hieroglyphs by Spanish writers at the time of the Conquest, and second by making comparisons with other known writing systems from places such as Egypt and Sumer.

Maudslay's interest in recording and deciphering Maya hieroglyphs reflected a growing concern with the hieroglyphs among both European and North American scholars, perhaps in emulation of similar studies in the Near East that blossomed in the early twentieth century. Despite the enormous fascination with hieroglyphics, only small progress was made in deciphering them until recently. The early archaeologists did manage to decode the Maya number system and its calendar, however. The number system was fairly simple, employing only three symbols: a dot for the value one, a horizontal bar for five, and a simple shell for zero. Combinations of bars and dots could express all numbers up to 19. For example, the number 17 was written as two dots over three bars. For numbers larger than 19, the Maya were ingenious enough to use place values, as our number system does, but few others. The Maya number system was based on the number 20 and used as "digits" the 19 numbers already described. The "digits" were written from bottom to top. The first and bottom place had a value of one; the next 20 (20 × 1); the next 400 (20 × 20); the next 8,000 (20 × 400); and so forth.

In contrast to their number system, the Maya calendar was incredibly complex, employing several interlocking cycles. One system of two permutating cycles was the Calendar Round of 52 years. The Maya identified each day by a combination of a name and a number from 1 to 13. Because there were 20 names and 13 numbers, 260 days could be named by this method, giving a 260-day period, the Sacred Round, as one fundamental unit of time. Meshing with the 260-day period was a second fundamental unit, the 365-day Vague Year, which was divided into 18 months of 20 days each, with an interval of 5 days added at the end. A particular day would have two dates: one from the 260-day period and one from the Vague Year. A day designated as, say, 1 Imix 4 Mac could not return until 52 years had passed. The Maya had another system for measuring larger eras of time, as we will see in the next chapter. By the turn of the century, scholars were able to roughly correlate Christian dates with those of the Maya.

But perhaps most important for our concern here, the preoccupation with Maya inscriptions reinforced the already conspicuous emphasis on the standing architecture and the elite culture, since the inscribed stelae had been produced by the Maya rulers and stood near their temples and palaces. Moreover, the great interest in the inscriptions focused attention on the Southern Lowlands during the Classic period, the region and period where and when the overwhelming majority of inscribed stelae were to be found. As we have already seen, this triad of elite, Southern Lowland, and Classic period aspects of

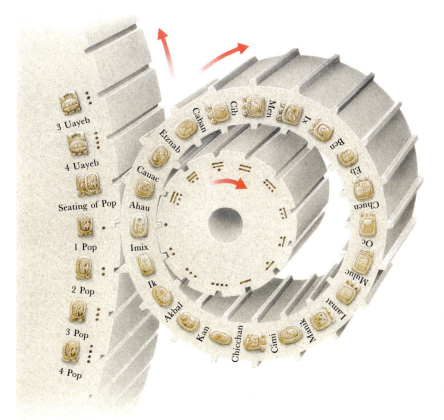

The interlocking cycles of the Maya calendar can be visualized as a set of intermeshing circular gears. The 260-day cycle is on the gear to the right, and the 365-day cycle is on the gear to the left. As the gears move, they indicate the successive pairing of days from each cycle.

ancient Maya civilization came to dominate much of Maya studies up until quite recently.

The dominance of this triad was reinforced by the excavations begun near the close of the nineteenth century. The first large-scale excavations of a lowland site were undertaken at Copán by the Peabody Museum, Harvard University, in the 1890s. Much of the excavation actually consisted of clearing the rubble and earth that had accumulated on top of large structures since their abandonment. This research produced a map of the large standing structures at the core of the site, which gave a better view than previously available of the overall layout of buildings and monuments at a Classic ceremonial center. In particular, it showed how truncated pyramids topped by temples, long multiroomed structures (dubbed "palaces"), and low platforms were arranged around open plazas. Carved stelae and altars were set in these open spaces or in front of the buildings.

When in 1912 R. E. Merwin of the Peabody Museum excavated a pyramid at the site of Holmul, he found for the first time evidence that a succession of buildings had occupied the same location. The archaeological constructions were arranged in so-called stratigraphic layers that, like geological strata, were dated from older to younger as the layers went from bottom to top. Merwin uncovered a series of elite burials in a number of rooms that had been constructed one after another over a long period of time, from the Preclassic through the Late Classic. Two of these burials were in specially built chambers underneath the floors of two superimposed rooms, labeled "tombs" in the drawing on the facing page. It became clear that many of the large standing structures in the lowlands were built up (and rebuilt) over a period of years. Unfortunately, Merwin's excavations were not published in full, complete with analyses of the whole ceramic vessels that had been placed with the burials as grave offerings, until 1933. Nevertheless, the widely known basic data contributed another useful piece to the growing picture of ancient Maya civilization.

Another important piece of research was the ethnographic study of modern Maya peoples conducted in the early twentieth century by Alfred M. Tozzer of Harvard University. Tozzer studied both the Yucatec Maya and the Lacandón Maya of Chiapas. Of particular significance was Tozzer's observation that many traits—especially rituals—in both groups had their origins in Precolumbian times. Tozzer compared modern cultural practices and linguistic terms with descriptions of Maya culture from the time of the Conquest and presumably

In this 1895 photograph of the Copán expedition, workers are removing carved blocks that have fallen from the Hieroglyphic Stairway.

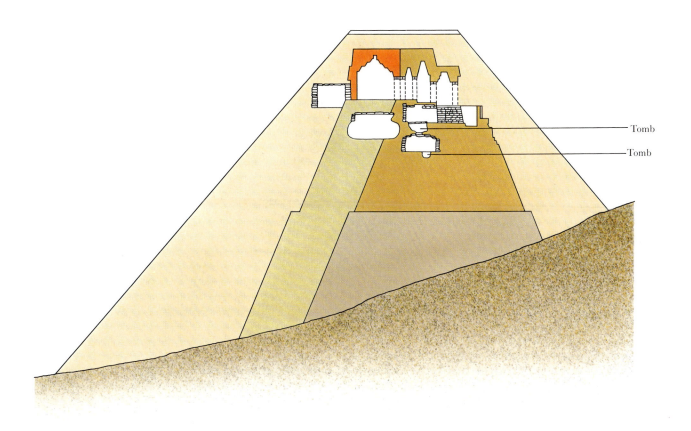

Tomb

Tomb

earlier contained in the early Spanish writings. For example, the Yucatec Maya still perform a rite for rain that appeals to the rain spirits or Chacs, just as the rites of the sixteenth-century Maya did. Tozzer's influential study reinforced the idea, already present, that aspects of modern Maya culture could serve as direct analogies to the past.

The first full-scale syntheses of Maya archaeology were attempted around the beginning of World War I. The early syntheses by scholars such as Thomas Joyce, Herbert Spinden, Thomas Gann, and Eric Thompson between 1914 and 1931 generally consisted of simple descriptions of Maya "history" based on the ranges of dates from hieroglyphic inscriptions found at different major sites and the historical sequence for the Northern Lowlands of Yucatán discussed in Conquest

This cross section of a pyramid excavated by Merwin at Holmul clearly shows how the Maya built one structure on top of another, often leaving the earlier structures virtually intact. The colors represent different building stages. The second stage, dates to the end of the Late Preclassic period and includes the two tombs lying beneath a floor. The vaulted rooms, which also contained burials, date to the Early Classic, and the outer structure is from the Late Classic.

This village belongs to the Lacandón, a Maya people who live in the tropical lowlands of Chiapas, Mexico. Ethnographic studies of modern Maya peoples have provided useful analogies for the interpretation of ancient Maya civilization. However, scholars now realize that such analogies should be viewed more critically than was the case in the past.

documents. These histories were little more than chronologies of the establishment and collapse of various sites and buildings. These historical frameworks were then "fleshed out" by ethnographic descriptions of the lifeways of modern Maya peoples. Implicitly or explicitly, archaeologists assumed that there was significant continuity from past to present, particularly in regard to everyday life.

The scholarly accomplishments of the four decades following World War I were tremendous. Numerous field surveys located hundreds of sites and mapped the locations of the principal standing stone buildings. Although some maps were more like quick sketches, others were carefully drawn plans. Many of the stone structures, particularly the temples and palaces, were in turn drawn and described in detail.

Many aspects of ancient Maya civilization that scholars accept as givens were uncovered from the late nineteenth century to the end of World War II, during the time the traditional model was being developed. Not only did archaeologists decipher the Maya calendric system and correlate it with the modern calendar, but they uncovered the nature of the Maya mathematical and astronomical systems. Many of the themes depicted in ancient sculptural, mural, and ceramic art were made known, and the nature of the Maya religious pantheon with all its many-faceted deities was disclosed.

UAXACTÚN

The keystone in the development of the traditional model of Maya civilization was the Uaxactún archaeological project, which was undertaken by the Carnegie Institution of Washington between 1926 and 1937. The study of Uaxactún was arguably the most important archaeological project until the University Museum's field research at Tikal in the late 1950s and early 1960s. It put much of the flesh on the bare bones of the prevailing model of the Maya that had first begun to emerge nearly a century before with Stephens' and Catherwood's travels.

Uaxactún is a moderate-sized center in the Southern Lowlands located just 40 kilometers to the north of the much larger site of Tikal. It was selected by Morley for investigation by the Carnegie Institution in part because in the 1920s the earliest known dated stela in the lowlands was located there and because the dated monuments indicated that it had had a long occupation. The research at Uaxactún was carried out in two phases, one from 1926 to 1930 and the other from 1931 to 1937. The first phase was directed by Oliver Ricketson and the second was overseen by A. Ledyard Smith.

As Ledyard Smith has noted, "Before the investigation of Uaxactún little was known about the Maya culture in the southern lowlands of the peninsula of Yucatán." With the publication of the major monographs describing the research at the site between 1937 and 1955 (along with a host of shorter reports), archaeological knowledge about the ancient Maya, particularly the elite, expanded dramatically. The Uaxactún research solidified the general understanding of various facets of elite culture that had already begun to be built up.

In the realm of architecture, for example, surveys and excavations at Uaxactún as elsewhere showed a clear pattern of construction and use of space, particularly in the Classic period. Rooms in Maya stone buildings usually had vaulted ceilings. The vaults were not true (or Roman) arches but were constructed so that the weight of the ceiling was borne by the walls in which the vault stones were lodged. This type of vaulting forced rooms to be high and narrow. Windows were uncommon. Structures usually were arrayed around plazas, both buildings and plazas having plastered floors.

The masonry of the Classic period at Uaxactún and other lowland sites featured finely cut stone blocks held together by lime mortar. Producing such stonework was time consuming and labor intensive. The limestone had to be quarried, carefully shaped and finished, hauled and lifted into place, and then precisely fitted with neighboring stones. Archaeologists contrasted this Classic block masonry with the veneer masonry of the Puuc region and elsewhere at the end of the Classic, which provided a beautiful exterior for rough interior hearthing. By the Late Postclassic, architecture was perceived as having deteriorated. On the exteriors of these very late buildings, thick coats of plaster made from local limestone hid unshaped interior stone.

The Uaxactún project perhaps made its most critical advance in the area of chronology. Archaeologists use changing ceramic and architectural styles from a variety of sites as means to date developments in a culture. To begin an analysis of ceramic styles, they gather thousands of examples from their architectural excavations at a site. For instance, the Maya used garbage, along with earth and rocks, as fill beneath floors and behind walls. The garbage included broken pieces of pottery, or potsherds. Potsherds—and when lucky, entire pots—taken from architectural fills, burial tombs, deposits lying on floors, or ceremonial caches would be classified into different types according to characteristics such as shape and decoration. Ceramics of the same type would be assumed to have been manufactured relatively closely in time.

Archaeologists are able to date the types by several methods. For example, a carved monument may belong with a particular architectural level. If the inscription on the monument has a Maya calendrical date in it, that date can be converted into a modern Christian date, and scholars will have the date of the level and everything in it. Or, a painted polychrome vase from a burial may have a Maya date painted on it, giving the exact date of the burial and all the offerings in it. Comparisons with dated materials from neighboring areas also can help fix points in the chronological sequence. By these means archaeologists were able to formulate dated sequences of ceramic types. Once scholars had defined the ceramic sequences, they could date the occupations of individual buildings and, by extension, whole sites. Through time, an overall sequence of development for the Maya lowlands was erected, spanning over two thousand years from Preclassic

The type of vault used by the ancient Maya, called a corbel vault.

through Classic to Postclassic. This sequence, albeit with some important modifications, is still the standard for Maya archaeology today.

Mayanists' understanding of chronology in the lowlands was clarified and solidified by the analysis of artifacts found at Uaxactún, particularly the ceramic analysis by Robert E. Smith (Ledyard Smith's older brother). As Ledyard Smith insightfully points out:

Probably the most important contribution of the investigation [of Uaxactún] was the ceramic study that resulted in the classification of the pottery into four phases covering the whole span of occupation of the site. It was now possible to distinguish between local and imported pottery and to get an idea of what outside contacts existed in the different periods. The ceramic sequence also was very helpful in establishing the architectural sequence at Uaxactún, starting in the Late Preclassic period and continuing through the Late Classic. These sequences, ceramic and architectural, made it possible for archaeologists in the future to assign the pottery and structures excavated at other sites to their correct chronological position.

The achievements of the Maya were now securely placed in time. Although the six hundred years of the Classic period were generally seen

These examples of Preclassic and Classic pottery were found during the excavations at Uaxactún. By comparing these pots with other pottery types or by associating them with dated architectural levels, Robert E. Smith was able to date the red bowl to the Middle Preclassic period, the cream dish to the Late Preclassic, the black bowl to the Early Classic, and the orange tripod plate to the end of the Late Classic.

From 1926 to 1937, archaeologists at Uaxactún were able to excavate a number of large elite buildings, including the important excavations of Structure A-V shown here.

as a monolithic unit, it was possible for the first time to divide it up into a number of well-defined subunits distinguished by stylistic changes.

In addition to refining Classic era chronology, the Uaxactún research clearly showed that the great Classic florescence at the site stood on top of an at least thousand-year-long Preclassic foundation. Although most of the evidence collected about this early period was restricted to potsherds found beneath the large Classic architecture, this finding at least conclusively showed that the Maya had been present in the lowlands for many centuries before the beginning of Classic civilization. Unfortunately, the nature of this Preclassic culture, aside from the characteristics of its ceramics, was not explored in any great detail.

The Uaxactún research gave Mayanists like Eric Thompson and Sylvanus Morley a more refined chronological framework to organize their recreations of Classic life. They also had much richer data about Maya culture than ever before. Yet their vision of the Maya was as much determined by what the Uaxactún researchers didn't find as by what they did. Many new research directions were initiated but not followed up or their significance not realized. As a result, data were missed that could have challenged the old model.

For example, in order to estimate the population of Classic Uaxactún, Oliver Ricketson undertook an innovative study of the remains of perishable houses surrounding its ceremonial core. In a path-breaking piece of research, archaeologist Robert Wauchope later excavated five examples of such remains and then undertook a comparative examination of modern Maya houses. Although Ricketson's study was an important step toward a broader understanding of Uaxactún, it did not go far enough away from the center to give him a full picture of the site's extent or population (he surveyed a cruciform-shaped area with arms 1600 meters long and 365 meters wide extending away from the center). Moreover, he simply counted mounds instead of analyzing their differences. He did recognize that not all the mounds were necessarily houses, but he had to rely on guesswork as to how many were. Wauchope's follow-up study was not organized so that he could test Ricketson's assumptions about how many and what kinds of mounds were houses. Furthermore, he downplayed variability among the five structures, and his sample was quite small.

There also was another sampling problem. Ricketson surveyed only a small part of the area surrounding Uaxactún. Without having any controls over his sampling universe, he had to assume that the zones immediately around the core were homogeneous, and therefore that his sample could be projected on the whole zone. While this assumption certainly was a fair one with which to start, it unfortunately was never examined, and its validity was taken for granted.

Another potentially important road not followed concerns the rise of the Classic period. One of the principal foci of investigation at Uaxactún was Structure E-VII, which appeared as a conical mound just under 15 meters high before excavation. This building faced east onto one of the plazas in the site. At the base of a stairway on its east side stood a carved monument, Stela 20, with a hieroglyphic date of 9.3.0.0.0 in the Maya calendar, which has been read as A.D. 495. A platform on the other side of the plaza served as a base for three small temples that faced west. Detailed measurements indicated that this plaza grouping had astronomical significance: an observer on the stairway of E-VII could see the sun rise on both annual solstices and equinoxes just over either one of the far corners of the two end temples or over the center of the middle one.

The very well preserved temple-pyramid that was found inside of Structure E-VII at Uaxactún, shown here in a drawing by Tatiana Proskouriakoff, was one of the first indications that significant public construction preceeded the Classic period.

While removing rubble from the sides of E-VII, excavators discovered an earlier structure. As the ancient Maya often built new constructions directly on top of older buildings instead of razing them, the earlier building—called E-VIIsub—had been completely covered by E-VII and was very well preserved. E-VIIsub was a truncated pyramid about 8 meters high and between 23 and 24 meters on a side. Stairways ascended in the middle of all four sides. Post holes on top of the structure indicated that it had originally been topped by a perishable building with wooden posts. Spectacularly preserved stucco ''grotesque'' masks were found flanking the stairways on the third (lower zone) and fourth (middle zone) levels of the pyramid, and two more were placed on the east side of the fifth level (upper zone). The eighteen masks are replete with symbols relating to Maya iconography and religion.

Although archaeologist Edith Ricketson's study of the ceramics found in E-VIIsub indicated that some predated the Classic period and that the building was early, it was not realized at the time that E-VIIsub possibly dated centuries before the beginning of the Classic period. The question of the growth of complex society at Uaxactún, in particular, and among the Maya, in general, did not become a major focus of research and was not considered in the light of the finding of E-VIIsub. In effect, although archaeologists noted the presence of monumental construction predating the rise of Classic Maya civilization, they virtually ignored the implications for labor organization, elite control, or a host of issues related to the processes of complex development.

Another significant contribution having unfulfilled promise was the incredibly detailed excavation by Ledyard Smith in Structure A-V, a building often called simply the Palace. Smith excavated over five field seasons from 1932 to 1936. He cleared all the earth and debris that had accumulated over the construction and then drove two huge trenches through the structure, from the east to the west and the north to the south. Descending from the top of the visible remains to bedrock, the trenches uncovered a complex but highly informative stratigraphic sequence of architecture. Structure A-V was actually a complex of buildings, built during twenty principal phases of construction covering the whole Classic period. Huge quantities of ceramics were found from all the phases, as were a number of burials and ceremonial caches.

The excavations revealed that the complex had begun as several stone house platforms, which would have supported perishable structures of wood and thatch. These platforms were later covered by a small platform supporting three temples near the beginning of the Classic period. Over the centuries this platform was transformed into a complicated group of multiroomed buildings with a series of inner courtyards. While the excavators clearly recognized that Structure A-V had probably changed over time from a primarily religious complex to an elite residential/"office" complex, archaeologists did not examine the implications of such a change. As was typical of the period, the change was described but no attempt was made to explain it—to ask why it had happened. Nor did archaeologists analyze the changing use of space, from the accessible early temples to the restricted access of the later "palace" complex. The possibility that the sociopolitical organization had altered between the Early and Late Classic periods was not explored.

During five hundred years, from the beginning
to the end of the Classic period, Structure
A-V was rebuilt several times, starting as a
simple platform with three small temples (top)
and ending as a large temple-palace complex
with inner courtyards (bottom). The original
platform in the first drawing lies under the
back courtyard of the second. Part of the
complex lies incomplete; construction was
apparently halted in midstream when Uaxactún declined in the ninth century A.D. These
reconstructions were drawn by Tatiana Proskouriakoff.

MAYAPÁN

Before it closed down the Division of Historical Research in 1958, the Carnegie Institution of Washington conducted its final major archaeological project at the Late Postclassic site of Mayapán in northern Yucatán between 1949 and 1955. Directed by Harry Pollock, the Mayapán research had a number of innovative components. Ethnohistorian Ralph Roys conducted a study of the historic documents pertaining to the site, and his results influenced both fieldwork and interpretations. The project also performed detailed, intensive mapping of the walled urban center and all the residences.

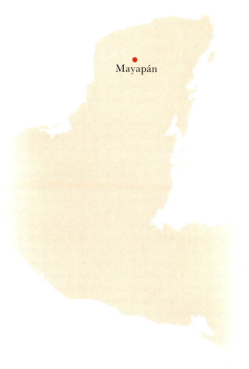

The heyday of Mayapán lasted approximately two centuries, from A.D. 1250 to 1450 (the Late Postclassic or Decadent period). After Chichén Itzá collapsed, Mayapán was the dominant center in northern Yucatán and the capital of a widespread political confederacy. The city had a compact urban form; its boundaries were defined by a wall enclosing 4.2 square kilometers. Twelve gateways allowed entrance into its walls. The Carnegie mapped about 4,000 structures in which lived 12,000 people according to project estimates. Within the city's walls were found twenty-six *cenotes,* or natural wells.

The highly nucleated and tightly defined urban layout was quite different from the more dispersed urban plans of earlier Maya cities. The closeness of the dwellings must have affected daily life and made necessary more social and perhaps governmental controls. The surrounding land was so poor that foodstuffs may have been imported to feed the populace. A system of collecting and redistributing food or of trading through markets may have been in operation, although no concrete archaeological evidence for such activities was uncovered. Residents may have contributed food for their own tables, as walls around many of the houses were interpreted to enclose gardens. The distinctive incense burners found at the site depicted anthropomorphic conceptions of the major Maya deities; parts of the censers appear to have been mass-produced, indicating a sophisticated organization of workshops.

Yet despite some innovative research, the general emphasis of the Carnegie project remained in keeping with the still-dominant traditional approach. The project still focused on the elite aspects of the site; excavators did not try to sample all the domestic structures but concentrated on the grander buildings and houses. The overall thrust of the observations was that Mayapán was the last gasp of a dying

This colonnaded structure from the heart of Mayapán reveals what until recently were seen as the "decadent" construction techniques typical of the Late Postclassic period. Instead of making the columns from carefully cut stone drums, the later Maya piled up rough stone slabs, which were held together with mortar. Originally, these columns would have been plastered over to look round, although clearly the quantity of labor invested in their construction would have been considerably less than needed for the cut stone columns.

civilization. The Carnegie reports stressed the crudeness of the architecture at Mayapán, as well as of the artistic and material inventory. The archaeologists' personal dislike of the architecture is clearly in evidence throughout the Carnegie writings, and their distaste heavily colored the interpretations of the center. As Ledyard Smith, a member of the Carnegie team, states, "A fact well demonstrated at Mayapán is that the high cultural standards of the Maya of the Classic period had sadly degenerated by the beginning of the fifteenth century." Smith goes on to say:

Stone carving and many of the arts deteriorated, owing to the unrest of the times. The architecture at Mayapán shows this degeneration as much as anything. There was evidently no time to waste on selecting fine-grained stone and cutting and facing it the way building stones were finished in the Puuc sites or at Chichén Itzá. Limestone was quarried without regard to quality, and was roughly shaped into blocks and slabs for building. In order to make the walls appear smooth, a heavy coat of plaster had to be applied. It was poor construction, and it did not withstand the destruction of time like the earlier, well-constructed buildings of the Classic period. There seems to have been little striving for permanence, just window dressing and false fronts.

Pollock also says, "That personal comfort and glory came ahead of religious devotion is shown by the palaces and finer residences being better built and apparently more lavishly furnished than the temples and other ceremonial buildings." An alternative, but apparently not seriously considered interpretation could have been that religious devotion was as strong as ever but expressed in different ways. Nor did it seem to occur to researchers that the ancient Maya of Mayapán were not looking for the approval of later archaeologists in their building but were constructing for the moment. The plaster-covered structures would have worked well at the time, even if they look relatively crummy today.

It is easy to decry the external flashiness of a McDonald's or a Holiday Inn and bemoan the architectural decadence that such buildings represent, but to people who can regularly eat out or travel with an ease that they did not have earlier, such judgments are beside the point. While an elitist assessment of the architecture of Mayapán is not "right" or "wrong," it certainly is not the only way to view the architecture. Moreover, "decadence" in architecture and art does not necessarily imply overall cultural decadence. Even in the 1950s, archaeologists from the Carnegie Institution of Washington were not only allowing their personal perspectives to uncritically affect their interpretations of the archaeology of Mayapán but also to limit their data collection and their studies of these data.

ETHNOHISTORICAL MATERIALS

A final source of data for the traditional model came from the analysis of both native Maya and Spanish documents from the sixteenth century. Archaeology has long used written records, where available, to expand understanding of artifacts and sites. Historical writings can often provide useful analogies for explaining the function of particular artifacts or buildings. For instance, documents describe the historical (and modern) Maya use of stone basins (*metates*) and oval stones (*manos*) for grinding corn. When archaeologists find stone basins and stones that exhibit striations indicating grinding, the historical writings provide a strong basis for interpreting the implements as metates and manos. When interpreting the Sacred Cenote at Chichén Itzá, archaeologists relied on sixteenth-century descriptions of the Cenote as a pilgrimage shrine and a place where occasional human sacrifices

An ancient Maya woman probably used a metate and mano to grind corn in the manner shown here.

were made. On an even larger scale, historical mention of the Island of Cozumel, off the east coast of the Yucatán Peninsula, as a trading and pilgrimage center provided part of the basis for the research strategy and some of the hypotheses of the Cozumel Archaeological Project of the early 1970s, of which I was codirector.

Yet, as much historical research has shown, archaeologists must approach the written record with considerable caution. It is a common dictum that history is often written by winners, whose reporting may be propaganda or may be heavily selective and highly biased. The form and function of artifacts also change, so that an artifact does not automatically have the same function as a similar form discussed historically. The links have to be carefully examined, not assumed.

Leaving aside the very recent decipherments of large parts of Maya hieroglyphic texts, perhaps the most important native documents for archaeologists have been the *Books of Chilam Balam*, particularly that of the town of Chumayel in Yucatán. In the *Books of Chilam Balam*, Post-Conquest Maya recalled their culture and history prior to the arrival of the Spanish. The books were written in the Maya language but transcribed in European script, and somewhat different histories were written down in different Yucatecan towns. Although written in the late eighteenth or early nineteenth century, long after the Conquest, these books reflect lore that was handed down among the Maya from generation to generation.

As the anthropologist Munro Edmonson, who has translated from Maya to English the *Books of Chilam Balam* from both the towns of Tizimin and Chumayel, has noted:

The *Books of Chilam Balam* (Spokesmen of the Jaguar) of the Yucatecan Maya constitute a treasure-house of historic and ethnographic information collected by the Maya themselves over a period of many centuries. They are exasperatingly difficult to translate and interpret for a number of reasons. They are largely composed in archaic and elliptical language. Their chronology is obscured by esoteric numerological, astrological, and religious assumptions. The orthography of the surviving texts leaves a great deal to be desired. But most of all the books reflect a world view and a sense of history that are distinctively Mayan.

The *Books of Chilam Balam* were probably most important for archaeologists because they offered an historical framework for the Postclassic period. The movement of groups, the conflicts between great families such as the Xius and the Cocoms, and the rise and fall of sites like Chichén Itzá and Mayapán and their political rivalries could all be tied in one form or another to chronological and geographic schemes of the five or six centuries preceding the Spanish Conquest. Although there was, and still is, much disagreement about how to interpret the historical materials, they nevertheless provided Maya archaeologists a foundation upon which to study the Postclassic period.

The most significant of the Spanish documents has almost certainly has been Landa's *Relación de las Cosas de Yucatán*. Bishop Diego de Landa arrived in Yucatán in 1549 and served as bishop there from 1573 to 1579. His interest in Maya culture led him to write down much of what he observed or heard during his travels and discussions with Maya. Ironically, the Church under his direction destroyed Maya written documents as "works of the devil," but Landa's own writings are the source of much information about the Maya at the time of the Conquest. For example, information about Maya hieroglyphic calendrics contained in Landa's book helped scholars equate the Maya and modern Christian calendars.

Although there had been numerous editions of Landa's writings since the original manuscript was first discovered by Abbé Brasseur de Bourbourg in Madrid and published in 1864, the one most widely used by archaeologists was Alfred Tozzer's heavily annotated version published in 1941. As Tozzer noted in his "Introduction" to the volume:

The source material presented by Landa includes practically every phase of the social anthropology of the ancient Mayas, together with the history of the Spanish discovery, the Conquest and the ecclesiastical and native history together with the first accurate knowledge of the hieroglyphic writing.

Many of the analogies used in traditional interpretations of data from archaeological research in the lowlands came from Landa's writings.

Even with all these different sources of information, in 1950 knowledge of the ancient Maya still was relatively limited. Yet we must remember how relatively short the history of Maya archaeology actually is. The first excavations in the Maya lowlands were not undertaken until less than one hundred years ago in the 1890s, while the Preclassic period was not well defined until the 1930s. Moreover, it was only about seventy-five years ago that the Maya calendar was

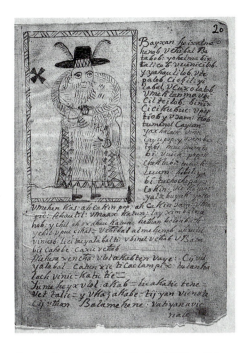

A page from one of the *Books of Chilam Balam*.

fully linked to the modern Christian calendar by Joseph Goodman, setting Maya history firmly in an absolute chronological framework.

Although knowledge of the lowland Maya was still limited, by the mid-twentieth century sufficient information was in hand for Eric Thompson and Sylvanus Morley to provide full-blown syntheses of the conventional wisdom about Maya civilization. These semipopular overviews of the subject remain the best expositions of the traditional model of the ancient Maya. In order to better understand the nature of this model and how it was formulated, we need to know something of Thompson and Morley's lives, their cultural environments, and their biases, as well as the general intellectual trends in the discipline of archaeology at the time.

J. ERIC S. THOMPSON

Rightly viewed as the "Dean" of Maya archaeology during his lifetime, Sir Eric Thompson (1898–1975) profoundly influenced the growth of Maya archaeology. After going through two editions, his superbly written *The Rise and Fall of Maya Civilization* is still read by scholars and tourists alike.

Born in London, Thompson served in World War I, where he was wounded in action. After the war, he worked as a gaucho on family land holdings in Argentina. He then returned to England and studied anthropology under A. C. Haddon at Cambridge. In 1926, he began his career in Maya archaeology, working for Sylvanus Morley at Chichén Itzá and then for the Field Museum of Natural History. From 1935 until his retirement in 1958, he undertook research in the Maya area for the Carnegie Institution of Washington. Thompson remained active after his retirement researching and publishing on Maya hieroglyphic writing and ethnohistory.

In keeping with the tenor of the times, which found archaeologists being very conservative in their professional articles and more speculative and "theoretical" when talking to general audiences, a real disjunction can be found between Thompson's scholarly and more popular writings. In the former, he tended to be much more cautious, although his strongly held opinions and assumptions can be found in both. It is in his popular writings that Thompson's championing of the traditional model came to the fore. In works such as *The Civilization of the Mayas* (1927 and many later editions), *The Rise and Fall of Maya*

The Thompsons (at the right) on their honeymoon, photographed with the Morleys at Chichén Itzá in 1930.

Civilization (1954, 1966), and *Maya Archaeologist* (1963), his view of Maya civilization is quite clear. More interesting, so is his projection of his own culture onto the Maya:

> The ceremonial center was the symbol of the small group of priests and nobles (the two were often indistinguishable) who ruled the peasants. . . . A rough comparison might be made with those old ecclesiastic principalities, such as Salzburg, with the archbishop ruler living in pomp surrounded by his cathedral, administrative buildings, nunneries and friaries, on which were lavished all the art of the age, or, from the religious and ecclesiastical sides alone, one can think in terms of an English cathedral close. Perhaps we shall not be too far from reality in regarding the Classic period, *mutatis mutandis* as a sort of exotic background for Maya cousins of Archdeacon Grantly, Mrs. Proudie, and Mr. Harding, not in top hats but in quetzal plumes, and sipping not the 1820 port—"it's too good for a bishop, unless one of the right sort"—but the native *balche*. Indeed, every important Maya ceremonial center might be viewed as a sort of tropical Barchester, and on a mural at Bonampak there is a splendid portrait of Mrs. Proudie watching the bishop at the seat of judgment. Only as long as the right sort were in control did the Classic period endure.

J. Eric S. Thompson continued to play a key role in Maya studies even after his retirement from active fieldwork.

Such "Victorian self-identification," as Kent Matthewson has called it, can be found throughout Thompson's writing. In fact, it has been noted that many of the leading Maya scholars in the first half of this century were themselves upper class or upper middle class in background and either unconsciously or unapologetically transferred their Western European elite values onto Maya culture.

Archaeologist Marshall Becker of West Chester University argues that Thompson's interpretations were heavily influenced by views of medieval life that were current in England of the 1920s. Becker notes that English society had clear class divisions and much class consciousness. According to the prevailing view at that time, the medieval period featured broad class divisions; scholars gave particular attention to cathedral construction by "inspired and toiling peasant volunteers directed by their priests." This perspective contrasts with the later and more complex view that emphasizes the significance of varied middle-class artisans. Becker concludes that Thompson transferred the simple, then-dominant view of medieval life to ancient Maya civilization. He also points to a fear and dislike of urbanism then present in English intellectual thought, which may explain the tenaciousness of Thompson's argument that ancient Maya cities were not truly "urban." Finally, Becker suggests that Thompson's hypothesis that the collapse of Maya civilization in the ninth century was caused by peasant revolt against the increasingly oppressive demands of their rulers reflects the fears of communist uprisings that were another feature of his intellectual circle.

Thompson not only projected his own background on the Maya, he also adopted a "see no evil" attitude toward the ancient people whom he so much admired. For example, he saw relations among centers as essentially peaceful ("I don't see too much bullying of a small city state by a big one"), although, as we shall see, there was a reasonable quantity of pictorial data, including scenes on carved monuments and painted murals, to indicate otherwise.

Thompson's admiration for the ancient Maya was much influenced by his contacts with their present-day descendants. An important turning point in the development of the conventional model occurred in the years from 1927 to 1929 when Thompson, while researching in southern Belize, became friendly with the Maya laborers for the archaeological projects, especially Faustino Bol from the village of San Antonio, who served as Thompson's guide. Thompson was very favorably impressed by the Maya. Moreover, he noted:

My contacts with our Maya workers from San Antonio and long talks with Faustino on our journeys had indicated that these modern descendants of the ancient Maya still preserved many ancient customs and religious ideas. This seemed to be a mine well worth working, so I decided that at the first opportunity I would stay in San Antonio, living just as the people there do, to learn everything that was possible about such survivals, for it was clear that archaeological excavations were not the only means of learning about the ancient ways.

Thompson's observations and impressions of the modern Maya clearly came to influence his views of the Precolumbian Maya, not only his identification of specific cultural traits but also his general interpretations of the ancient civilization.

Thompson's superbly written popular books not only influenced general readers but also had a major impact on professional thinking. Thompson's intellectual stature, his encyclopedic knowledge of the Maya, and his persuasive writing style all contributed to the enduring and uncritical acceptance of his ideas—an impact that has influenced Maya archaeology for more than sixty years and is still felt today more than a decade after his death.

SYLVANUS G. MORLEY

The great Mayanist Sylvanus G. Morley (1883–1948) also had a profound impact on the conventional interpretation of ancient Maya civilization. In particular, his book *The Ancient Maya*, first published in 1946 and recently reissued in a fourth revised edition, has guided and affected the thinking of many of its abundant readers. Morley attended Harvard, where he studied under yet another influential Mayanist, Alfred Tozzer. After a series of expeditions to Maya sites, he became a research associate of the Carnegie Institution of Washington in 1915 and subsequently undertook further surveys of the Southern Lowlands. He later directed the huge Carnegie project at Chichén Itzá from 1924 to 1940.

A young Sylvanus Morley in his trademark sombrero stands next to a huge "zoomorphic" altar at Quiriguá.

Like Thompson, Morley was especially interested in Maya hieroglyphics. He spent much of his life looking for hieroglyphic inscriptions, recording those inscriptions, and attempting to decipher their contents. Through Morley's efforts, the corpus of known Maya centers and carved monuments increased dramatically between the two world wars, and the archaeological map of the lowlands began to be filled in with new detail. He was able to locate new stelae by asking for help through posted advertisements, which were answered by local residents and chicle workers who tapped trees to supply gum for the companies that produced commercial chewing gum.

Although the hieroglyphic system was only partially deciphered at the time they were working on it, both Morley and Thompson believed that the inscriptions were concerned exclusively with calendrics, time, astronomy, and other religious concerns such as the complex deities who made up the Maya pantheon. On the other hand, they strongly felt that the inscriptions did not record more mundane, historical matters, such as the births, deaths, and other activities of the elite. As Norman Hammond has stated, "Their agreement on this topic bottled up progress in decipherment for a generation." With most attention focused on calendrics and other esoteric concerns, it was not until the end of the 1950s that breakthroughs by Heinrich Berlin and Tatiana Proskouriakoff on the historic content of some inscriptions, along with linguistic advances, allowed scholars to reach a new understanding of a number of glyphs.

Even though Morley's views of the ancient Maya differed from those of Thompson in certain specifics—Morley, for instance, saw the Maya centers as more complex entities than did Thompson—their models of Classic civilization were essentially similar. Both shared the highly subjective mode of interpreting the remains of Maya civilization that was typical of archaeologists of their era. In addition, both stressed the erudite achievements of the Maya and the religious preoccupations of the elite.

Sylvanus Morley's numerous expeditions in the lowlands searching for new glyphic inscriptions, as well as his long-term research at Chichén Itzá and residence there, brought him into regular contact with modern Maya. Like Thompson, his strong emotional bonds with the Maya heavily influenced his interpretations of the ancient Maya. And like Thompson, Morley was an unabashed lover of all aspects of the ancient Maya world. Just read the last paragraph of *The Ancient Maya*:

When the material achievements of the ancient Maya in architecture, sculpture, ceramics, painting, lapidary work, feather work, and cotton weaving and dyeing are taken into consideration, and, further, when to these are added their abstract intellectual accomplishments, such as the invention of writing and positional arithmetic with its concomitant development of zero (certainly unique for the New World), the construction of an elaborate calendar and chronology (the latter with a fixed point of departure and slightly more accurate even than our own Gregorian calendar), plus a knowledge of astronomy superior to that of both the ancient Egyptians and the Babylonians, and then finally, when their cultural attainment is judged in the light of their *known cultural limitations*, which were on a par with those of early Neolithic Man in the Old World, we may safely acclaim the ancient Maya, without fear of successful contradiction, as the most brilliant aboriginal people on this planet.

In brief, he consistently emphasized the distinctive and peerless nature of Maya civilization.

I have discussed in some detail the impressions, analogies, and conclusions that dominated the thinking of two great Maya archaeologists. They saw parallels to European and Classical elitism and class structure in the remains they studied in the lowland rainforests, and for more than forty years of this century the popular vision and explanation of Maya civilization came, in large part, from the perspectives of these two giants.

THE INTELLECTUAL UNDERPINNINGS OF THE TRADITIONAL MODEL

In pointing out the subjective biases of Thompson and Morley, I am merely reviewing the background for the development of the traditional model. I do not mean to imply that their views are wrong or unacceptable because of their obvious lack of objectivity. Archaeologists today understand that previously held notions of pure scientific objectivity in the study of the past are simply untenable. They realize that archaeological research is unarguably affected by the theoretical and subjective outlooks of its practitioners.

A good example of such effects can be found in the archaeological research at the site of Sayil in the Puuc region of the Northern Lowlands. Between 1983 and 1988, my colleagues and I undertook the first

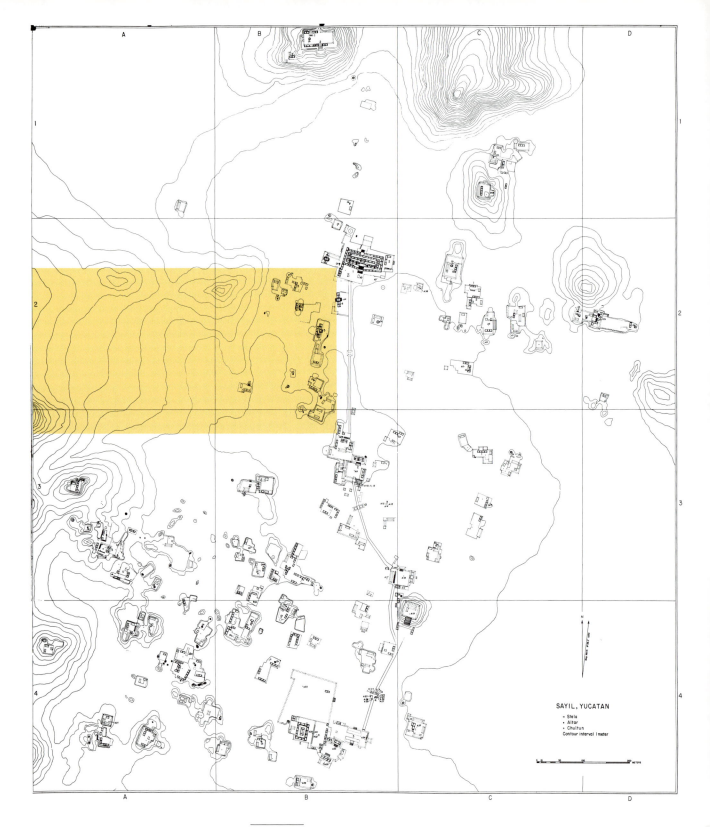

SAYIL, YUCATAN

- Stela
- Altar
- Chultun

Contour interval 1 meter

N

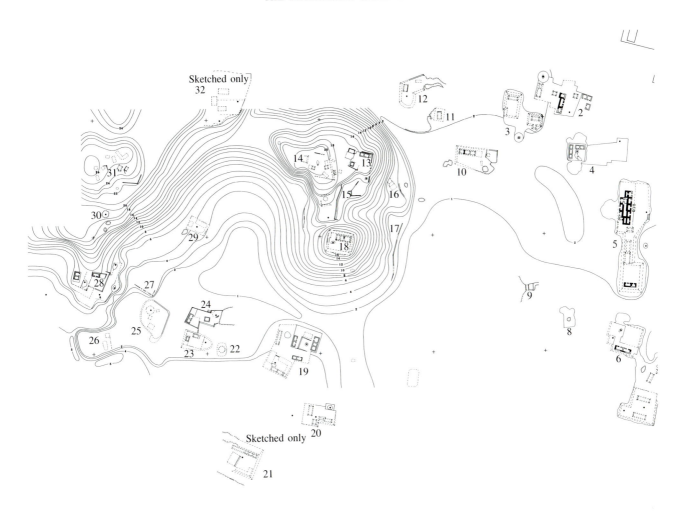

Sketched only
32

Sketched only

Edwin Shook's 1934 map of Sayil, a superb map for the time, locates the substantial stone buildings (left), but he ignored the less conspicuous ruins. The area inside the color rectangle is almost empty in Shook's map, while in the recent mapping of Sayil (above) that same area was found to be filled with structures.

intensive settlement pattern study in the Puuc region at Sayil. We mapped all visible human-made features on the landscape and related them to their natural topographic setting. We cleared a number of areas within the site from which we collected materials, and we excavated a wide range of structures. We mapped well over two thousand features ranging from large stone buildings to the remains of small perishable wood and thatch houses. Our results showed that between A.D. 800 and 1000 Sayil was densely occupied: perhaps nearly 10,000 people lived in the urban core of 4.5 square kilometers, and an additional 7,000 lived in the zone surrounding this core.

Ours was not the first widescale map of the site. In 1934, Edwin Shook, working with Harry Pollock, both of the Carnegie Institution of Washington, mapped the substantial stone buildings in the center of the site. Shook saw the remains of many of the less substantial, perishable structures but did not include them on his map. In a 1980 publication, Pollock is forthright in his description of the mapping procedures. Time was at a premium, so only what were considered the most "important" features were mapped. Pollock states, "The maps of Sayil

The two-story South Palace at Sayil is a good example of the kind of elite structure that traditional archaeologists preferred to investigate. This Terminal Classic building is located to the west (left on the map) of the end of the causeway in the bottom left-hand corner of Edwin Shook's map of Sayil on page 58.

and Labná are incomplete in that they omit a good number of small constructions. . . . we tended to exclude the inconspicuous building remains from our architectural studies." He notes that "many small structures that presumably were dwellings are not shown on the map." In sum, given the elite perspective of the day, the non-elite structures were ignored.

Or, as a hypothetical example of the effect of bias, in past years if an archaeologist who firmly believed that the ancient Maya were peaceful found a number of spearpoints, he or she might immediately interpret them as hunting implements. The archaeologist could then continue to argue that there weren't any material indications of Maya warfare. The points or their place of discovery would not be tested to see if the function of the points could be more firmly determined, although such tests would not be too difficult to set up. For instance, the archaeologist might hypothesize that hunting implements would be found in domestic contexts and war weapons in public ones. Then he or she could design a research strategy that would sample these contexts in the field.

Remains such as these of a well-preserved perishable domestic structure at Sayil would have been ignored when ceremonial centers were mapped prior to the 1950s. Here, a worker is clearing the floor of the middle room of a three-room building. The visible stone foundation originally supported wooden walls and a thatched roof. The building might have resembled the drawing on page 79.

Archaeologists are coming to understand that the problem of validating archaeological conclusions and testing hypotheses is a problem of methodology. Thus, while biases cannot be eliminated, they need to be recognized. Assumptions should be made explicit and inferences separated from "facts." For example, although Morley loved to make assertions like "the ancient Maya loved their children deeply, just as their descendants do today" and treated these sentiments as accepted facts, we now know that such statements about ancient cultures cannot be easily verified and are simply opinions.

A growing number of archaeologists have concluded in recent years that scientific procedures should be employed in formulating and testing hypotheses, instead of using assumptions, made from unsupported analogies, as "explanations." We can see, in other words, that the problem was not with Thompson's and Morley's conclusions themselves, but the way in which they were reached. Thus, in the past, Eric Thompson could declare:

An interesting illustration of how a knowledge of present-day beliefs and customs can be used to interpret archaeological practice came my way some years ago. I had found in a votive cache on the summit of a pyramid at San Jose an incense burner and two bones which turned out to be the ear bones of a manatee. I couldn't imagine why the Maya should have attached ear bones of that queer sea mammal and published the find without comment. Years later, C. M. Barber, director of a museum in Flint, Michigan, told me that sixty years ago he had found the natives of Maya descent around Lake Izabal, Guatemala, regard the ear bone of a manatee strung on a cord around the neck as a magical protection for the wearer. He thought that was because the manatee's sharp hearing is its best defense. He had surely hit the nail on the head and from his observations given the correct interpretation of an archaeological find.

While the interpretation is surely "interesting" and may well be "correct," we do not know whether it is an accurate or useful inference given Barber's and Thompson's highly informal manner of reasoning. Up to the last two or three decades, such modes of reasoning were the accepted procedures.

Another illustration can be found in Thompson's assumption that the Classic Maya had markets. This assumption is a particularly critical one because it has a host of implications for the economic and political organization of ancient Maya cities. Thompson, however,

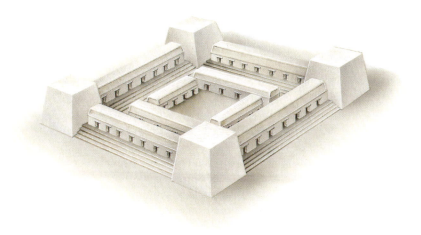

never supported or further clarified his assumption about markets. Unfortunately, there is little positive archaeological evidence even today to support claims for markets at Maya sites. What would a Maya market look like in the archaeological record? To reason that (1) the Maya *must* have had markets, (2) markets are held today in large open areas, and (3) this open area at the ancient Maya site under investigation *must* have been where a market was located, is typical of the kind of methodologically weak thinking that characterized much of archaeology through the 1950s, as well as the conventional model of the Maya.

We can only assume that Thompson's assertion about the presence of markets at Classic centers is based on analogy to the modern Maya in the Guatemalan highlands, who have large, well-organized markets. But reasons for thinking that this kind of cultural behavior has a long continuity were never offered, and ways of testing for the presence of markets were just not considered. The assumption of markets was just one of a number of unarguable "givens" that were symptomatic of the prevailing norms of archaeological practice in the Maya area.

Why did such transparently impressionistic, anecdotal explanations endure for so long as the "authoritative" interpretations of ancient Maya lifeways? The archaeologist Norman Hammond of Boston University has argued that "as the Classical Archaeology of the New World, it [Maya archaeology] shared with the study of Greece and

This featureless, enclosed quadrangle is the kind of space that has often been labeled a marketplace in the archaeological literature on the Maya. The complex lies to the east of the Great Plaza in the center of Tikal. Based on current published information, it is sheer speculation as to whether or not this space was in fact a market.

Rome an *embarras de richesses* of architecture, art, and inscriptions, which kept its practitioners immersed in fact long after those less well endowed materially had been forced to seek new ways of interpreting their material." However, there were problems even in the use of "facts" in the traditional model. Unsupported inferences were treated as givens, and archaeological data were often interpreted by stipulation (recall, for example, the equation of open plazas with market-places). These stipulations were then in turn treated as facts ("the ancient Maya had markets," instead of "the ancient Maya might have had markets; how can we pursue the validity of such a possibility?"). Once anecdotal explanations were accepted as "facts," the problems of interpretations were compounded when further inferences were made based on the original, potentially faulty assertion. Morley, for instance, argues:

Relying upon archaeological evidence, such as minor differences in the sculpture, architecture, and ceramic wares of the different parts of the Old Empire region, which indicate a corresponding number of archaeological subprovinces, we may perhaps go even farther and hazard the guess that each of these archaeological subprovinces originally corresponded roughly to a politically independent city-state.

From then on, this assumption ("guess") is treated as a fact upon which further inferences are made. Moreover, the guess hinges on an important assumption which itself is never examined. Do "minor" stylistic differences necessarily indicate "subprovinces"? This assumption actually is an important hypothesis of questionable validity that warrants explicit definitions and careful testing, not casual acceptance.

Finally, it should be noted that until the 1960s, Maya scholars were not only unconcerned with methodological issues, they were relatively uninterested in theory and explanation, too. While their discussions of ancient Maya civilization were replete with much detailed archaeological information, they rarely asked explanatory questions, such as, What caused the rise of ceremonial centers and why did they expand? What role did the environment play in the growth of complex social and political organization? How did the rise of cultural complexity in the Maya lowlands fit in with general theories of cultural development? As the eminent anthropologist Clyde Kluckhohn noted back in 1940, "I should like to record an overwhelming impression that many students in this field are but slightly reformed antiquarians. . . . there seems to be a great deal of obsessive wallowing in detail of and for itself." He goes on to say that "factual richness and conceptual poverty are a poor pair of hosts at an intellectual banquet." Thus, although concerned with *what* the Maya developed, archaeologists evinced relatively little interest in *why* or *how* the Maya developed what they did.

By the end of World War II or shortly thereafter, the data to be used first by Morley and then by Thompson in their general overviews of ancient Maya civilization were in place. Many of these data had been uncovered by the Carnegie Institution of Washington, which employed Morley and Thompson for long periods of time. As the archaeologist W. W. Taylor, a student of Clyde Kluckhohn's at Harvard and, until his retirement, a professor at Southern Illinois University, pointedly noted in a landmark but highly controversial book, *A Study of Archaeology,* published in 1948 before the research at Mayapán:

Both the field work and the publications of the Carnegie are weighted overwhelmingly toward the hierarchal. They have hardly touched, and then only incidentally, the cultural remains of the common Maya. But even within the hierarchal culture, the emphasis has not been to construct a picture of how the Maya hierarchy lived: what they did and where, when, how, and with what. Such intensive excavations as have been made have not been directed toward the clarification of these problems, but rather toward the finding of material for comparative and chronological studies or, many times, just to excavate a structure which appeared to be of a rare or unknown type or was prominent or artistically beautiful.

Taylor further said that "merely making physical descriptions of architecture, ceramics, and cities and placing them in chronological order . . . is chronicle. . . . What Carnegie has been doing is really chronicle of a restricted range of Maya culture: the artistic, religious, and epigraphic remains of the hierarchy." Unfortunately, Taylor's arguments did not have any real effect on Maya studies until more than a decade later when, as we shall see in the following chapter, new research at the huge site of Tikal and shifting methods of archaeological investigation brought major changes to Maya studies.

NEW
VIEWS
OF
THE
CLASSIC
PERIOD

*A portion of the Bonampak murals depicting
a Maya leader and his retinue.*

$\mathcal{J}$n the 1960s and early 1970s, new field research and analyses were producing results that could no longer be accommodated by the established model of Maya civilization. The traditional wisdom came under concerted attack, and by the mid-1970s, the old model had been replaced in the professional literature by a new one. Within a decade, the new views were being introduced to a wider, popular audience in books such as *Ancient Maya Civilization* by Norman Hammond, *The World of the Ancient Maya* by John Henderson, and the fourth edition of Morley's *The Ancient Maya*, prepared by Robert Sharer. In this chapter, I will examine new data revealing that the Classic Maya culture was not as idyllic, yet more vital and inventive, than archaeologists had imagined.

Some of the new data were simply the result of the quickening pace of field research in the Maya lowlands beginning in the 1950s. Many of the new data, however, were obtained through advances in the methods employed by Maya archaeologists. Trace element analyses of artifacts, radiocarbon dating, and faunal, floral, and soil analyses proved to be valuable techniques. But perhaps the innovations most critical to the growth of the modern view of Maya civilization were new techniques of remote sensing and an improved methodology of settlement pattern studies.

SETTLEMENT PATTERN RESEARCH

Studies of ancient settlement patterns have done more to change archaeologists' views of the Maya than any single new procedure. A pioneer in settlement pattern research was Gordon R. Willey of Harvard University, who in 1953 published his classic work *Prehistoric Settlement Patterns in the Viru Valley, Peru*. Willey defined settlement patterns as "the way in which man disposed himself over the landscape on which he lived." He used the term to refer to the nature and arrangement of the dwellings and other buildings in community life. Willey believed that settlement patterns would supply important clues about the technology and the institutions of social interaction and control that had shaped those patterns.

Before Willey, only the centers of sites were mapped, because that was where rose the standing stone architecture. Even within the mapped zones, relatively small traces of human occupation were ignored, particularly where no stone architecture was visible. The entire

survey often consisted of mapping easily observed standing structures, then asking local workmen if they knew of any other buildings or carved monuments in the vicinity. A trail would be cut to a structure that the workmen knew, it would be mapped, and a trail would be cut to the next one, and so on. One has only to compare site maps before the 1950s with those made later to see how great a difference the new procedures made. And, I am only talking about the mapping stage here, not the subsequent collecting, excavating, and analysis!

In contrast, Willey's strategy was to carefully map first all human-made features visible on the landscape within a set area, be it the confines of a valley or an arbitrary distance well beyond the site center. A small platform just centimeters off the ground that once supported a perishable house was just as fair game as a large standing stone building. The mappers would carefully record the principal aspects of the natural environment, such as water sources, topography,

Gordon R. Willey, the modern "dean" of Maya archaeology, is standing with his arms folded at the center of the back row in this 1954 photograph, taken inside the excavations of mound BR-1 at the site of Barton Ramie in the Belize River Valley.

and soil types. Once the mapping was completed, archaeologists would look at the survey maps for patterns. To give two simple examples, they might find that specific kinds of buildings occurred with certain soil types or that a particular type of structure was placed only along a river or canal.

In Willey's final step, archaeologists would search for analogies that could assign possible functions to the pattern. Suppose that archaeologists were investigating an environment having patchy pockets of rich soils. They might find that modern peoples in similar environments have a pattern of scattered settlements that resembles the archaeological example: perhaps peasant farmers live nearby the good soils, those who don't farm live on the poorer soils, and large storage structures are located in the zone of poor soils for stocking foodstuffs that will be distributed to the population at large. Once the functioning of this modern example had been examined and explained, archaeologists would devise tests to see if the analogy explains the archaeologically uncovered settlement pattern. Thus, detailed settlement mapping reveals the relationships of kinds of structures to other kinds of structures and ultimately to features of the natural environment, yielding clues to the deeper significance of such patterning.

After developing his strategy while in Peru, Willey shifted his attention to the realm of the Maya. In the early 1950s, he began a settlement pattern project at Barton Ramie in the Belize River Valley, and by the end of the decade several new settlement pattern studies were underway at Dzibilchaltún in the Northern Lowlands and at Tikal and Altar de Sacrificios in the Southern Lowlands. Willey's new approach was critical to Maya archaeology because of its focus on *all* dwellings, both elite and non-elite, its concern with relating structures to the physical environment, and its attempt to infer function for the structures mapped.

The detailed mapping at Barton Ramie quickly revealed the presence of large numbers of non-elite domestic structures (so-called housemounds). The researchers soon realized that excavations of these mounds could produce useful information about ancient Maya lifeways. The first mound that Willey and his team excavated in 1954 was numbered BR-1. Willey described the excavation as follows:

The mound was revealed to be a successive accumulation of superimposed platforms and floors which has sustained rather simple perishable structures. Outwardly a rounded, domelike hillock, these superficial contours of recent humus accumulation were stripped back to expose a rectangular stone-faced, clay-filled, and plaster-and-gravel-floored platform. This platform, on being cleared away, disclosed another of similar form with a terrace attachment and so on to the bottom of the mound and the original ground surface. The earliest platform or house foundation, constructed without mounding, was of circular form with an adjoining rectangular terrace or extension. Throughout the excavation, at all levels, burned clay wattles or briquettes with pole-mark impressions, ash, sherds and stone artifact fragments, and other debris were found on floors and in the intervening clay between floors.

The archaeologists also found simple graves under the floors of the houses. They found that settlements were concentrated on natural terraces slightly raised from the river bottom, and they noted that houses were regularly spaced about 50 meters from each other. From examination of the density of settlements and its relation to soil type and terrain, they were able to make inferences about agricultural practices and crops. The spatial relationship of the houses to a small ceremonial center also allowed them to speculate about local political organization.

The earliest level of the BR-1 mound at Barton Ramie revealed the remains of a perishable house having a circular shape and a rectangular extension.

Up to the 1950s, it could reasonably be claimed, as did Walter W. Taylor, that Maya archaeology "hardly touched, and then only incidentally, the cultural remains of the common Maya." With the methodology of settlement pattern study firmly in place by the 1960s, such a statement was no longer tenable.

Clearly, the meticulous techniques of modern settlement research have greatly increased the time needed to map Maya sites, let alone excavate samples. This is especially true given the difficult vegetation that must be tackled and all the logistical problems of working in the Maya lowlands. Obviously, the increased time has meant greatly elevated expenses. Yet the return of information for investment has been unanimously deemed worthwhile by workers in the field.

Willey's settlement research finds its direct intellectual source in the fieldwork and writings of one of the great cultural anthropologists of the twentieth century, Julian H. Steward, who at the time of his death in 1972 taught at the University of Illinois at Champaign-Urbana. Steward's research in the American Great Basin and Southwest during the 1930s convinced him that his contemporaries were wrong in their belief that the environment was neutral in cultural development. He pioneered the study of cultural ecology, which tries to understand the interaction between the environment and culture. Steward introduced settlement pattern studies as one way to investigate human-environmental dynamics.

Although Steward and Willey introduced settlement pattern studies to American anthropology, European archaeologists had been concerned with settlement and the environment much earlier than their North American colleagues. The delay in the Americas almost certainly has to do with the American reaction against the intellectual excesses of cultural evolutionary and environmental determinist thinking of the late nineteenth century. Some cultural evolutionists and determinists of that period had used such thinking to justify Eurocentric and racist interpretations of history. For example, some argued that the environment of Western Europe was the most conducive in the world to the development of the "highest" cultures. Until Steward, Americans firmly resisted any form of reasoning that suggested the environment played an active role in culture change.

My newly completed research at Sayil illustrates how a typical settlement survey would be performed today in the Maya lowlands. During the five-year archaeological project, my colleagues and I spent three field seasons just making the settlement map. To cope with the

This trail is part of the survey grid that was cut by the Sayil Archaeological Project through dense forest.

thick, overgrown forest cover that blankets most of the site, we set up a grid system of survey blocks a hundred meters on a side. Because the thick vegetation often made it impossible to look from one feature to another over any considerable distance, the grid system was needed to help us locate features on our map and systematically organize our survey. Local Maya workmen cut trails with machetes along all of the arms of the grid, whose starting (zero) point was located just off the corner of the three-story Great Palace that dominates Sayil's urban core. We were fortunate that the Carnegie Institution of Washington had earlier mapped many of the large stone structures, sparing us the effort.

The impressive Great Palace is the largest building at Sayil.

A mapping crew at Sayil. One archaeologist is working the EDM theodolite, a second one is drawing a map from the readings given to him by the first, and a local Maya worker is holding the reflecting prism over an archaeological feature.

Our regular mapping procedure called for archaeologists to walk through each grid block at 25-meter intervals, sketching in rough form the features on each side. A second survey crew followed equipped with an EDM "laser" theodolite. This "total station" surveying instrument has a built-in electronic distance meter. The instrument sends out an infrared beam to a prism that reflects the beam back to the instrument, which calculates the distance and height of the prism and displays those measurements in an LCD readout either directly or after the raw data have been punched into a built-in minicomputer. This second crew first cleared the area of larger vegetation and then meticulously measured the archaeological features using the theodolite. Local workmen held the survey rod with the mounted prisms and positioned them at the corners of platforms and other structures. The distance readings gave the dimensions of the structure, the angles of its sides, and its position on the map. The surveyor on the instrument called off the distance and height readings from the microcomputer on the theodolite to another archaeologist who immediately drew them on a map. In this way, all the features were tied to the grid. The crew also took elevation readings of the changing terrain in order to prepare contours for the site map—a part of the survey that can supply significant information about the correlation of settlement features with the landscape. We found, for instance, that house platforms were often associated with small natural rises, which apparently were the best location for the digging of underground cisterns that stored water for the ancient inhabitants of Sayil.

Finally, a third team equipped with Fortran sheets reexamined all the features and coded their attributes (size, height, number of rooms, construction techniques, isolated artifacts, etc.) to form a data base that would complement the map. We then prepared the final contour maps at a scale of 1:1000, showing all the features in relation to the landscape. We also undertook a reconnaissance well beyond zones that were mapped in detail. Incidentally, our survey showed that the number of house platforms dropped off precipitously on all four sides of the site—although there were lots of irregularities owing to the natural features of Sayil's valley. We could infer that the probable boundaries of the urban zone enclosed an area of about four-and-a-half square kilometers. Although the technology employed at Sayil is more advanced than that available to earlier projects, older settlement surveys followed similar kinds of procedures using plane table mapping or even simpler pace and compass techniques.

RESEARCH AT TIKAL

The downfall of the traditional model began with the detailed settlement survey carried out by the Tikal Project of the University Museum, University of Pennsylvania. This path-breaking project studied the great site of Tikal in Guatemala from 1956 to 1970, first under the direction of Edwin Shook and then, for most of the life of the project, William R. Coe. Although the project expended much of its effort examining elite activities at the site's very center, studies of Tikal's environs produced many new and challenging data. Even the more customary elite-oriented research cast doubt on established thinking by bringing to light new information, such as the existence of major architectural developments in the Late Preclassic period.

The University Museum chose to make Tikal the object of a major archaeological campaign because of its overwhelming size. Tikal was the largest known site in the 1950s, in both the size of its individual structures and the number and spread of large buildings. Temple I, for example, towers more than 44 meters above the jungle floor, and the major structures at the center of the site cover an area of more than 4 square kilometers. Archaeologists felt that a protracted

Tikal

examination of Tikal could answer many of the key questions facing Maya archaeology, such as the Preclassic origins of Maya civilization, the functioning of Classic society, the great sites as ceremonial centers or cities, and the causes of the Classic collapse. As William Coe noted, "The biggest would be the best, given the problem at hand."

The size of the project was designed to match the size of the site. With its unprecedented resources and support, the Tikal project dwarfed earlier efforts. More than one hundred scholars worked at Tikal during the life of the project from 1956 to 1970, and research by the Guatemalan government continues there today. These researchers found more than one million potsherds, as well as other artifacts numbering in excess of one hundred thousand.

Temple II at Tikal in 1962 prior to its restoration.

The Tikal archaeologists in the late 1950s and early 1960s were still like pioneers as they expanded the frontiers of knowledge about the Maya. The construction of an airstrip by the Guatemalan government in a sparsely populated tropical rainforest, the building of a camp, and the crating in of supplies were difficult but exhilarating tasks. Even though Tikal had been explored for decades and even though the University Museum archaeologists had numerous well-articulated expectations, they were clearly surprised by many of the exciting discoveries. Just the clearing of the site center in the first few field seasons was tremendously elating, as new buildings, some quite large, turned up with electrifying regularity. New carved stelae were discovered early on, as were several reservoirs and important arrangements of buildings, like the widespread twin pyramid complexes. The first excavations revealed large-scale Preclassic architecture and un-covered the long ceramic sequence, stretching over a millennium and a half, that the excavators had predicted. Moreover, the clearing and intensive mapping rapidly alerted archaeologists that the occupation of the site had been much denser and had covered a wider area than had been anticipated.

The archaeologists' reactions are perhaps best summed up in William Coe's comment that he was "captivated" by Tikal. He says, "It is commonplace to speak of the splendid proud Maya, of their almost deified cities. Yet, such clichés are given renewed meaning—even superlatives, however florid, seem justified—when one stands in the midst of Tikal, or looks from a high temple doorway across the jungle that conquered the city and its Maya." But instead of leading to the subjectivity of the past, this sense of wonder helped launch an assault on conventional ways of looking at the ancient Maya.

Probably the field research that most significantly challenged the older views was the mapping and excavation of the remains of set-tlement outside of the central elite core of Tikal, which took place between the late 1950s and early 1960s. While the Tikal settlement survey did not employ any significant new technological innovations, it was the first settlement survey of a large Maya center. The survey combined Willey's general methodology with the detailed urban map-ping previously pursued at Mayapán in the early 1950s. The mappers intensively surveyed the 16 square kilometers surrounding the core of the site, where they found thousands of mounds of all sizes. Excava-tions in a number of these mounds suggested that many, if not most, were the remains of perishable domestic residences. After clearing the

The excavation at Tikal shown here revealed part of a foundation of a perishable house. The archaeologist William Haviland directed a program of intensive excavations of domestic structures in the 16-square-kilometer urban center of the site.

earth that had accumulated over the centuries, the archaeologists found a variety of domestic debris and evidence of low walls and floors, which were easily interpreted as the remnants of houses with from one to several rooms, including kitchens and other specialized activity areas. On the basis of simple analogies to historic and modern houses in the lowlands and depictions of houses in ancient Maya art, it was concluded that the structures originally had been made of wood and thatch.

The broken pieces of pottery discovered in these excavations were carefully analyzed. Archaeologists grouped potsherds into a large number of types and subtypes based on similarities in attributes. They categorized pots according to the form (jar, bowl, plate, etc.) and the design (motifs could range from simple circumferential lines to complex natural scenes). They also judged the surface color (red, black, polychrome, etc.), surface manipulation (incising, grooving, molding, etc.), surface finish (waxy, glossy, or plain), paste (the nature of the clay used to make the vessels), and temper. (The final characteristic refers to the materials like ground-up bits of limestone that ancient potters added to the paste to provide strength and stability to the clay during its manufacture and firing.) Archaeologists then looked for pots of similar types in analyzed collections from other Maya sites like nearby Uaxactún. Because the Uaxactún pottery types had already

This reconstruction of a non-elite domestic group shows what the ancient wood-and-thatch houses probably looked like. If left undisturbed over the centuries, the architectural remains of such a group would consist of the stone platform and the stone foundations of the houses. A compound such as this would have been lived in for many generations by an extended family.

been defined and placed in a detailed chronological ordering, a matchup between the two sites would give the age of a Tikal potsherd. The pottery found in the housemounds turned out to cover more than 1,500 years, from the eighth century B.C. to the ninth century A.D. Thus, individual housemounds had probably been lived in for long periods of time, sometimes many centuries, and large numbers of these houses apparently were occupied at the same time.

The mapping of Tikal immediately brought into question several of the most basic tenets of the traditional model. First, the older view of the non-urban ceremonial center was untenable. During the Classic period, a sizable population, estimated at 10,000 to 11,000 people, resided in the 16 square kilometers around the site core. When surveyors sampled selected areas in the surrounding zone (covering 63 square kilometers), they also found a high density of housemounds. For this larger area including the site core, the population of Tikal by the beginning of the Late Classic period in A.D. 600 is projected at approximately 39,000 people, and perhaps another 10,000 lived in the hinterlands around the site. Clearly, Tikal was no vacant center!

Second, if large numbers of people were living in and around Tikal, then all the assumptions about the Maya agricultural system were brought into question. Studies of modern slash-and-burn agriculture in lowland environments show that it can support population densities no higher than 160 to 320 inhabitants per square kilometer. However, the new Tikal settlement surveys indicated densities on the order of over 600 per square kilometer. The conclusion that some intensive agricultural techniques were practiced was inescapable, as was the possibility that crops other than the "great triumvirate" of maize, beans, and squash had been grown. Likely additions to the Maya diet include breadnut, an orchard crop, and manioc, a root crop.

Given the urban appearance of Tikal's settlement, archaeologists could sensibly argue that the earlier notion of a basic two-class system consisting of a small group of elite and a large group of peasants was much too simple. Archaeologists working at Tikal, such as William Haviland of the University of Vermont, inferred that if Tikal was indeed a city, then it must have had a number of workers creating other products besides food. The presence of large quantities of obsidian cores and chipping debris with particular groups of housemounds indicated that the inhabitants were stoneworkers. Evidence of other possible craft specialization, such as woodworking and ceramic manufacture, reinforced the hypothesis that the Maya socioeconomic system

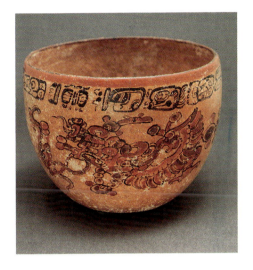

This bowl accompanied the burial of a woman at Tikal. By comparing it with dated ceramics from other sites, scholars were able to date this vessel to the early part of the Late Classic period, about 650 to 700 A.D.

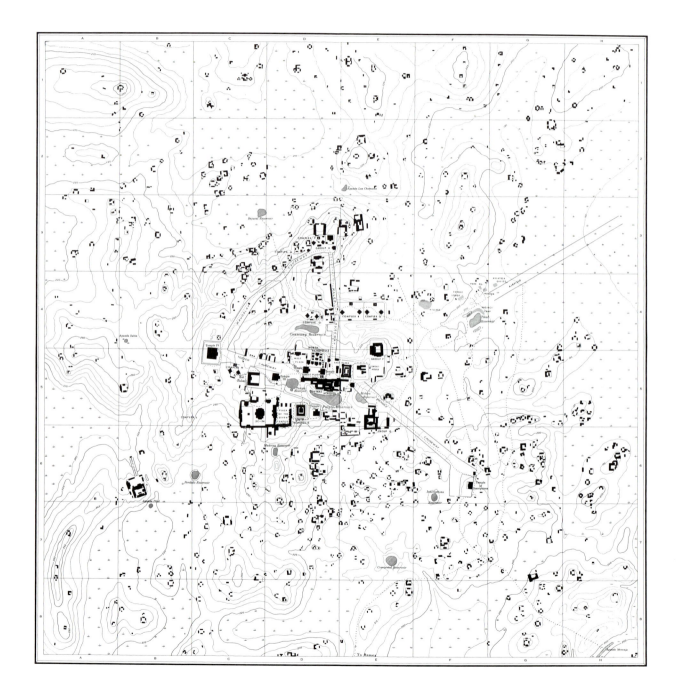

was more complicated than previously believed, although the data often were slim and archaeologists could not discriminate between full-time and part-time specialization.

AGRICULTURE AND REMOTE SENSING

While aerial photography had first been used in the Yucatán as far back as 1929 when Charles Lindbergh flew over the lowlands, it was not as important a part of Maya archaeologists' technological arsenal as it was for archaeologists in other parts of the world. The thick vegetation in most zones made it difficult to pick out whole sites, let alone individual structures. Aerial photography was only employed occasionally to look for new sites or for sites that had been seen on the ground in the past but had been "lost." Not until the 1960s and 1970s did its use become more sophisticated, as the technology both of taking photographs and of examining them improved significantly. In particular, scholars began to take advantage of aerial photography to examine the nature of ancient Maya agriculture.

The innovative settlement pattern studies had uncovered population densities that challenged the traditional view of the ancient Maya as exclusively slash-and-burn farmers. If more intensive forms of agriculture were practiced to support the large populations, what were they? When scholars reexamined earlier studies in search of data that might have been overlooked, they discovered that evidence of terraces and raised fields had been reported over forty years ago. Although the evidence was there, it was not realized until recently that the Maya were apparently able to mold the land to their own needs.

Evidence of ridged fields and canals was revealed in aerial photographs taken by the geographer Alfred H. Siemens of the University of British Columbia along the Candelaria River. Ridged fields are ridges of land that have been artificially raised above the river floodplain so that they will not be inundated during the rainy season. By this means, it becomes possible to farm the rich floodplain soil used to build and renew the ridges. The canals not only bring water to drier zones, but nutrients from the richer soils near the river. Both technologies allow farmers to practice intensive agriculture—that is, to farm year after year on the same plot—instead of having to shift fields as demanded by slash-and-burn practices.

Facing page: Robert Carr and James Hazard first published this settlement map of the central 16 square kilometers of Tikal in 1961. The Great Plaza with Temples I and II is located at the center of the map. Raised causeways radiate out to the west, north, and southeast.

Siemens and Dennis Puleston later verified on the ground ("ground truthed") that the canals and ridged fields did indeed exist. Although recent research has shown that at least some of these canals were built in historic times by loggers to float mahogany to waiting ships, the initial findings helped stimulate further research. Additional evidence for canals, for example, was uncovered by Ray Matheny at the site of Edzná in Campeche. Photographs also pointed to ridged or raised fields (a form of swamp reclamation) in northern Belize–southern Quintana Roo, Mexico.

At Pulltrouser Swamp in northern Belize, Peter Harrison of the University of New Mexico and B. L. Turner II of Clark University established for the first time that the Maya had practiced widespread swamp reclamation. Excavating along the margins of the swamp, they found unequivocal evidence of canals surrounding artificially constructed fields that extended from the natural shoreline into the swamp. The Maya had used the muck from the bottom of the canals to build up the reclaimed land. These human-built plots were incredibly fertile and could have produced multiple crops year after year. Microscopic studies of the working edges of stone axes found at Pulltrouser Swamp showed that they probably were used in the preparation of the artificial fields as tools for digging up soil and cutting vegetation. Harrison and Turner demonstrated that cultivation was particularly in-

Clearly visible in the center of this aerial photograph are ancient artificial raised fields in Pulltrouser Swamp, which extend from the shore into the swamp at the top.

tense during Late Classic times, although the beginnings of intensive agriculture were traced to the Late Preclassic period.

Maya archaeologists have been able to ascertain what crops were grown in the raised fields or other ancient agricultural zones by using flotation, a procedure that separates lighter materials such as seeds or pollen grains from soil samples. Simple flotation involves skimming off the lighter remains from the surface of the water into which a soil sample has been deposited. More complicated flotation devices make use of water and chemicals. Such techniques are especially significant in the Maya lowlands, where the moist environment has poorly preserved floral and faunal materials, as well as other perishable remains such as cloth, except in special circumstances such as in sealed tombs or in the Sacred Well (*Cenote*) at Chichén Itzá. Studies using flotation, as well as analyses of ancient pollen, have confirmed that maize was the principal crop of the Maya.

In recent years, breakthroughs in nonphotographic imaging of the earth, such as satellite imaging and side-looking airborne radar (SLAR), have had important applications in archaeology. These new techniques, along with aerial photography, are now collectively known as remote sensing. Side-looking airborne radar was put to good use between 1977 and 1980 by archaeologists R. E. W. Adams of the University of Texas at San Antonio and T. Patrick Culbert of the

The remains of an old raised field at Pulltrouser Swamp stand surrounded by artificial canals. Excavations by Peter Harrison and B. L. Turner II have confirmed that the fields and canals were not natural features.

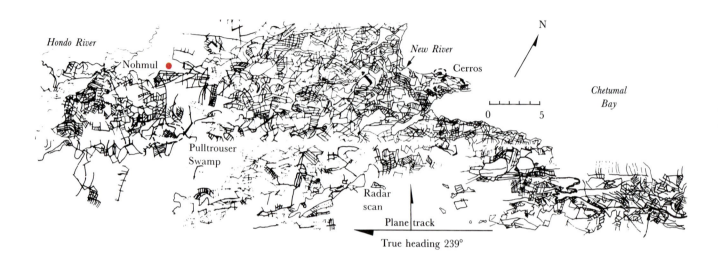

Some of the patterning left by possible canals in northern Belize has been revealed in radar imagery and confirmed in part by ground checking.

University of Arizona and radar scientist W. E. Brown, Jr., of the Jet Propulsion Lab. An airplane carrying their radar instrument flew at an altitude of 24,000 feet over much of the Southern Lowlands. This particular instrument had been developed by NASA to take pictures of the surface of Venus through dense clouds, so it is not surprising that it could penetrate the heavy tree cover of the tropical rainforest. The pictures showed a complex series of lines in different parts of the Southern Lowlands. Limited ground checking revealed that at least some of these features were canals used to irrigate fields along the floodbanks of several rivers. By means of sophisticated remote sensing surveys such as this, coupled with aerial photography and follow-up fieldwork, archaeologists were able to show how the great Maya centers could feed their large populations by practicing a variety of intensive forms of agriculture.

THE EVIDENCE OF WARFARE

Surveys of the more peripheral areas surrounding Tikal shattered the traditional perception of the Classic Maya as a basically peaceful people. (As the archaeologist Thomas Gann once stated in 1937, "The Maya . . . were one of the least warlike nations who ever existed.") Ditches running along long, narrow, artificial ridges, or parapets, were found approximately 8 kilometers to the south of the site center and 4.5 kilometers to the north, between Tikal and the large neighboring site of Uaxactún. The ditches and parapets ran for a total length of more than 9 kilometers. The Tikal archaeologists, particularly Dennis Puleston, suggested that these works had been used to defend Tikal from attack. The implication was clear: warfare may have played a greater role in Classic times than had been hitherto imagined.

Although well-known carved monuments and painted murals depicted military encounters between centers, traditional archaeologists generally regarded such scenes as evidence only of intermittent and unimportant raiding. The results of a battle or raid are illustrated by the beautiful painted murals of Bonampak on the western border of the lowlands, which were first reported in the late 1940s and published

The beautiful murals found on the walls of a palace at Bonampak are a rich source of evidence on the Late Classic elite. In this copy of a portion of the murals, a ruler in his jaguar pelt jacket stands in the center of the rectangular scene flanked by his elaborately garbed retinue. Nearly naked prisoners cower below, and a severed head lies two levels below the ruler.

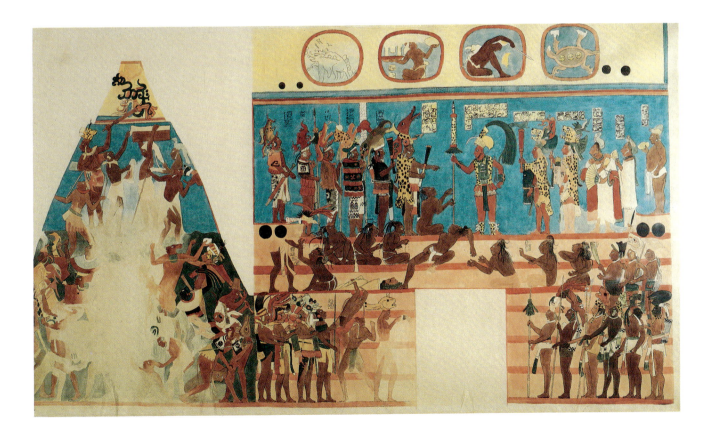

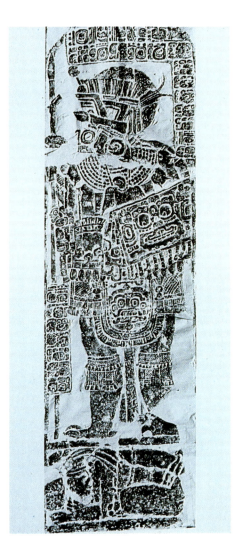

A Maya ruler stands on top of a bound captive in this rubbing taken by Merle Green Robertson of a stela at the site of Aguateca in the Petexbatún region just south of the Pasión River. This is just one example of many depictions of captured prisoners.

in monographic form in 1955. The murals portray captured Maya arrayed before their captor; one captive is already beheaded. Numerous stelae and carved panels from other sites also show captors towering over bound prisoners. Such depictions were usually considered to be of little moment, particularly since their violence ran counter to prevailing views of ancient Maya thought and behavior.

Eric Thompson gave his view of the harmony in Maya life when he stated:

Maya philosophy is best summarized in the motto, "Nothing in excess," which was inscribed over the temple of Delphi. Harmonious living, moderation, and a full comprehension of that spirit of toleration for the foibles of one's neighbors contained in the expression "live and let live" characterize the present-day Maya.

Thompson made it clear that, based on the surviving Maya writings, his perspective applied to both ancient and modern Maya. Thus, the popular view through the mid-1960s, as articulated by Thompson, was that "the absence of fortifications, the fact that most classic centers are in open country, and little evidence of warfare (the Bonampak murals of fighting rather clearly show a raid, not regular warfare) argue for an assumption of prevailing peace during the Classic period." The discovery of the Tikal earthworks is just one element of a counterargument that has been gathering strength in the past two decades: namely, that warfare and conflict were significant in the history of the ancient Maya.

Other recent findings strongly contradict Thompson's statement that "the ceremonial centers of the Classic period occupy open sites with no walls or bastions." The archaeologist David Webster of Pennsylvania State University has noted that possible fortifications have been identified at a number of sites. Webster has been the leading exponent of the hypothesis that warfare played a key role in Maya development, which is supported by his own research at Becán. The site of Becán is surrounded by a ditch and parapet. The parapet is about 5 meters in height, and the ditch is over 5 meters in depth and 1.9 kilometers in circumference. Archaeologists had known Becán since the 1930s, and even Thompson recognized that "Becán is a counterthrust to the argument I have been developing that large-scale warfare and fortifications are due to Mexican influences [at the end of the Classic period]." He contended, however, that the fortifications at

The ditch and parapet surrounding Becán are clearly visible in this aerial photograph.

Becán were in fact constructed at the close of the Classic period, while Harry Pollock hypothesized that the parapet and ditch were actually not fortifications at all but a "borrow pit"—a place where earth was dug up for construction purposes, or a kind of quarry. Given the biases against recognizing conflict in the Classic Maya world, Pollock's conclusion was reasonable.

Webster's fieldwork has subverted the arguments of both Thompson and Pollock. Although it was not possible to date the fortifications directly, the dating of structures and deposits that could clearly be linked with the parapet indicate that the ditch and parapet could not have been built any later than Early Classic times (about A.D. 300–600) and probably were built earlier in Late Preclassic times (about A.D. 100–250). Webster also showed that the argument that the ditch was a borrow pit was not a strong one, although some of the materials excavated from the ditch could have been used for construction at Becán. Webster argues that given the local geology, the ditch would not have been an effective means of quarrying. Moreover, much more material was removed from the ditch than could have been used in any construction project at the site. Finally, materials from the ditch were piled up on the inside lip of excavation to form an embankment but not on the outside lip, which would have been expected if the ditch had simply been a borrow pit.

A reconstruction of the fortifications at Becán based on the field research of David Webster.

The whole problem of fortifications is complicated by the fact that archaeologists cannot be sure how battles were carried out, and therefore just what role fortification may have played in conflicts. Although there are data from Conquest times on warfare, whether they apply to the Preclassic and Classic Maya is not certain. What information we do have from these sources and from Maya art does indicate that individual combat was a crucial component of war.

A breakthrough in the decipherment of Maya hieroglyphs highlighted the importance of conflict in the Classic Maya world. In 1960 Tatiana Proskouriakoff of the Peabody Museum, Harvard University, translated a glyph that appeared on monuments with captor/captive motifs as "capture." The archaeologist Joyce Marcus of the University of Michigan was able to argue in a 1974 article entitled "The Iconography of Power" that captor/captive motifs were a significant part of Classic Maya art. Marcus suggested that captor/captive scenes were used to symbolize and strengthen the political power of the captors. She went on to say that "themes of prisoners or military triumphs characterize early Mesoamerican states, perhaps especially during periods when they wished to appear in possession of powers which were not yet completely secure and institutionally effective." To arrive at her conclusions, Marcus carefully analyzed the corpus of monuments showing captive figures that had been discovered, photographed, and published through the years, many quite a long time ago. Since 1974, new information from sites like Dos Pilas and Quiriguá has strengthened Marcus' original argument. Hieroglyphic inscriptions and stone carvings from the former, for instance, reveal the presence of considerable conflict in the Pasión River drainage area during the Late Classic period, including the capture and killing of the ruler of Seibal by Dos Pilas.

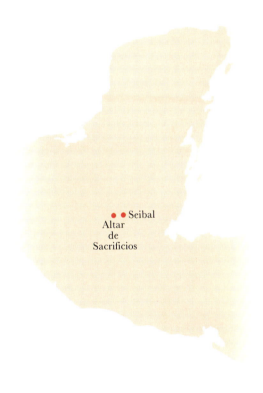

Altar de Sacrificios
Seibal

The conquest of the cities of Altar de Sacrificios and Seibal was unveiled by research directed in the late 1950s through late 1960s by Gordon Willey and Ledyard Smith of the Peabody Museum, Harvard University. Altar de Sacrificios sits at the juncture of the Pasión and Usumacinta Rivers on the western border of the Southern Lowlands, and Seibal is found upstream on a bluff overlooking the Pasión. A wide array of data indicate that non-Classic Maya peoples from the Gulf Coast lowlands had invaded these centers by the beginning of the ninth century A.D. These peoples have often been called Chontal Maya or Putun; they spoke a Maya language but were not part of the Classic Maya civilization. Evidence of the invasion came from ceramic analyses in particular, first by the archaeologist Richard E. W. Adams at Altar de Sacrificios and then by Gordon Willey and myself at Seibal, where I worked as a graduate student for four field seasons from 1965 to 1968. A foreign pottery that appeared to originate in the Usumacinta drainage in or near the Gulf Coast lowlands was found in quantities at both sites, while designs on some pieces were closely related to foreign figures and motifs on the Seibal stelae. Some foreign elite pottery types replaced locally made forms at the two sites.

A host of information indicated that Seibal was taken over by a foreign elite who deposed the indigenous Maya rulers. One strong clue

This masked face of a non-Classic Maya figure appears on a stela from Seibal dated to the ninth century. The speech-scroll emanating from the figure's mouth is an example of a feature definitely foreign to Classic Maya art.

was that in the figures and hieroglyphs on monuments, foreign traits became stronger through time. Facial features, dress, and ornamentation all appear to be non-Classic. We also found a monument showing a Classic figure offering obeisance to a foreign one. In addition, there is clear evidence that foreign architectural styles were introduced. The placement of a small pyramid with veneer instead of block masonry in the center of one of Seibal's plazas and a large round structure with an altar supported buy two Atlas-like figures are two examples of foreign architectural features. William Sanders of Pennsylvania State University and Barbara Price of Columbia University have argued that large-scale ceremonial architecture of a foreign style could not have been built unless the foreign power had secured control over the surplus labor of the local population. The changing use of space may also indicate a foreign influence. A settlement survey in the peripheries of Seibal showed that religious activities became centralized at this time. Outlying temples were abandoned, and the center of ceremonial and bureaucratic activities shifted from one central area of the site to another. There was a change in the kinds of incense burners used, yet domestic pottery continued unchanged, as did the domestic settlement

pattern. Both Seibal and Altar de Sacrificios flourished briefly under the aegis of the invaders, at a time when many other Classic centers in the Southern Lowlands were being abandoned.

Because these incursions occurred near the close of the Classic period in the Southern Lowlands, traditionalists could argue that they differed from normal Classic patterns. Nevertheless, the incursions did indicate that military invasions were one of the complex processes that led to the "collapse" of many Southern Lowland centers in the ninth century.

Webster posited in a 1977 article on "Warfare and the Evolution of Maya Civilization" that, as is the case in other early civilizations, warfare was a key variable in the social and political development of the Maya lowlands. In an argument that I find generally convincing, he maintained that warfare was a result of population pressure, which led to competition for resources in the lowlands as early as the Late Preclassic period (about 300 B.C.). Although Webster's argument is still debated, older notions of the peaceful Maya are clearly not tenable. Competition for resources and labor, and perhaps for markets for goods, probably incited conflict throughout ancient Maya history.

Both the placement and the style of this small pyramid at Seibal show a foreign influence. Its position in the center of the South Plaza defies the Classic Maya tradition of placing buildings only along plaza edges. And unlike Classic Maya structures, which were constructed of block masonry, this pyramid uses veneer masonry, formed by putting thin flat stones over a rough core. The pyramid, in the midst of reconstruction, dates to the early ninth century and is surrounded by Terminal Classic stelae.

THE CONTENT OF HIEROGLYPHIC INSCRIPTIONS

In the late 1950s, scholars began to make new breakthroughs in the understanding of Maya hieroglyphs. Because they found pronouncements of raids on neighboring centers, their work was another challenge to older conceptions of peaceful Maya. But more important, the new insights conclusively overturned Thompson's and Morley's firmly held convictions that the inscriptions reflected solely esoteric concerns. For it turned out that the glyphs had important historic content.

The archaeologists and epigraphers Heinrich Berlin and Tatiana Proskouriakoff made the first two pioneering strides in deciphering historic information. In 1959 Berlin was able to identify what he termed "emblem glyphs" in texts carved on monuments. He was the first to realize that these glyphs were the symbols of particular centers. After this breakthrough, other scholars could begin to pin down the historic messages in the inscriptions by establishing that certain actions were taking place at center *x* or were carried out by center *y*.

The emblem glyphs of six cities in the Southern Lowlands.

Tikal

Yaxchilán

Palenque

Seibal

Copán

Quiriguá

Shield Jaguar

Bird Jaguar

In 1960 Proskouriakoff made the crucial discovery that a variety of texts at the Usumacinta River sites of Piedras Negras and Yaxchilán recorded dynastic sequences or successions. At Yaxchilán, for example, she found that an individual denoted by the symbols "Shield Jaguar" ruled at the site in the early eighth century A.D. He was succeeded on the throne by "Bird Jaguar," who began his rule in A.D. 752. Other scholars set off to look for similar inscriptions elsewhere with spectacular success. At Tikal the art historian Clemency Coggins of the Peabody Museum, Harvard University, was actually able to work out a kinship chart tracing the generations of rulers from the time of the founder of the Tikal "dynasty" through much of the Classic period. She was also able to link some of the rulers with particular tombs. Moreover, she and others were able to show that the texts talked about marriage alliances and relations between centers. As Proskouriakoff said, "In retrospect, the idea that Maya texts record history, naming the rulers or lords of the towns, seems so natural that it is strange it has not been thoroughly explored before."

Proskouriakoff's innovative research forced Thompson himself to make a complete about-face. As Joyce Marcus has pointed out, in his

Left: Shield Jaguar (left) receives battle gear—including a jaguar headdress—from his wife (right) prior to a conflict on February 12, A.D. 724, according to Linda Schele and Mary Ellen Miller's interpretation of this portion of a carved lintel from Yaxchilán. *Right:* The glyghs for two rulers of Yaxchilán: Shield Jaguar (top) and his successor Bird Jaguar (bottom).

The noted archaeologist, epigrapher, and artist Tatiana Proskouriakoff, photographed at Piedras Negras in 1936.

1950 landmark work on Maya hieroglyphs, Thompson forcefully stated:

It has been held by some that Maya dates recorded on stelae may refer to historical events or even recount the deeds of individuals; to me such a possibility is well-nigh inconceivable. . . . I conceive the endless progress of time as the supreme mystery of Maya religion, a subject which pervaded Maya thought to an extent without parallel in the history of mankind. In such a setting there was no place for personal records for, in relation to the vastness of time, man and his doings shrink to insignificance. To add details of war or peace, of marriage or giving in marriage, to the solemn roll call of the periods of time is as though a tourist were to carve his initials on Donatello's David.

A little more than two decades later, he gracefully admitted that "work has shown that the generally held view, to which I subscribed . . . regarding the impersonality of the texts is completely mistaken."

Since the breakthroughs of the late 1950s and early 1960s, there have been a whole series of advances in scholarly understanding of the glyphs. Recently, the decoding of Maya hieroglyphs has made giant

A translation by Christopher Jones of a portion of the hieroglyphic text on a Late Classic stela from Tikal.

The day 13 Ahau
Eighteenth day of the month, Cumku,

End of the seventeenth katun.
The completion of its period.

[Part of the ruler's name?]
Chitam

In the dynastic line, lord of Tikal, [A title]

The ninth plus twenty,
In the count of the rulers

[Successor to?]
His lord father,

Yax Kin Caan Chac
[A probable title,]

In the dynastic line, lord of Tikal,   In his fourth katun [period of 20 tuns, or 360 day years]

The leader [batab]
Sixteen days plus one period of twenty days,

Plus two tuns [back to],
The day 11 Kan,

Twelfth day of the month of the parrot, Kayab,
He took the throne,

At the place of leadership,
He who scatters blessings.

strides through the use of phonetic analyses. In the past, most scholars assumed that all Maya glyphs were logographs, pictorial characters that stood for complete ideas or words. Yet as far back as the nineteenth century, some scholars supposed that Maya glyphs were at least partially phonetic—that is, some of the glyphs represented sounds and not concepts. The pioneer of modern phonetic research in Maya studies was the Russian scholar Yurii Knorosov. Using the alphabet that linked Spanish and Maya symbols published by Bishop Landa in his *Relación de las Cosas de Yucatán*, Knorosov was able to make a strong argument in the late 1950s that the Maya writing system was a mixture of logographs that represent whole words, such as the emblem glyphs, and phonetic symbols that stand for sounds. These phonetic symbols represent the sound of entire syllables. When strung together, they spell out words in the spoken language, just as our alphabet does.

Building on Knorosov's insights, a group of scholars, including, among many others, Floyd Lounsbury, David Kelley, Linda Schele, Peter Matthews, Steven Houston, and David Stuart, have made considerable progress in understanding Maya symbols. Nearly two-thirds of the estimated 800 hieroglyphics found on Maya stone monuments and pottery have been decoded, including about one-third of the 60 or so phonetic symbols. The deciphering of Mayan inscriptions has illuminated topics as diverse as Classic politics and the contents of elite ceramic vessels. Soon the inscriptions promise to reveal much about the lives of ancient Maya rulers.

THE CORRELATION OF THE MAYA CALENDAR

The Maya carefully recorded precise dates from their calendar in many hieroglyphic inscriptions. Recently, a scientific innovation has allowed archaeologists to confidently support a specific correlation of the Maya and Christian (Gregorian) calendars and thus give Christian dates to Maya dates that were carved on monuments during the Classic period. The innovation is radiocarbon or carbon-14 dating.

Carbon-14 dating has had a major impact on the field of archaeology since its invention four decades ago. One indication of its importance is that its inventor, Willard Libby, won a Nobel Prize for his discovery. The technique provides absolute dates for organic materials. When such materials can be directly associated with archaeological artifacts, the latter can be dated, too. Using results from thousands of dated contexts, archaeologists have constructed a worldwide chronological timetable for a huge variety of sites and cultures from the Late Pleistocene more than 40,000 years ago to recent times. Its impact on Maya studies, while much less important, has nevertheless been far from negligible.

Carbon-14 dating measures the remaining quantities of a radioactive isotope of carbon in once-living things like wood, human or animal bone, and shells. The technique tells when the organism died, or, in the case of wood, when the material presumably was transformed into a tool or structure. Carbon-14 atoms enter living organisms through photosynthesis and digestion, and leave by excretion, respiration, or disintegration. As a result of the continuous intake and loss of carbon-14, all living organisms have a constant proportion of the isotope among the much more numerous carbon-12 atoms. When an organism dies, clearly it is no longer able to exchange carbon with its surroundings. Because the carbon-14 already inside the organism continues to disintegrate at a known rate, the ratio of carbon-14 to carbon-12 can be used to determine the time since death (although such factors as sunspots, burning of fossil fuels, and explosions of atomic bombs can cause some difficulties with these determinations).

One of the great intellectual achievements of the Maya was the invention of a method for reckoning time labeled the Long Count (or Initial Series). The Long Count is just one aspect of the very complicated Maya calendar, which contains a host of cycles including periods of 365 and 260 days. The Long Count started counting time from what appears to have been an arbitrary point, a specific date about 5,000 years ago. Each Long Count date consists of a *baktun* (400-year unit), *katun* (20-year unit), *tun* (1-year unit), *uinal* (20-day unit), and *kin* (1-day unit) that have accumulated since the starting date.

By the time of the Spanish Conquest, the Maya had ceased to use the Long Count but were still using the Short Count (or Calendar Round) of 52-year cycles. A correlation between a Short Count date and a date in A.D. 1539 was made in a Spanish document from after the Conquest. The question for Mayanists was, to which point in the Long Count did these dates correspond? At the beginning of this century Joseph Goodman made a correlation between the Maya and Christian calendars, which because of later modifications by Juan Martinez and Eric Thompson is known as the Goodman-Martinez-Thompson or G-M-T correlation. These three argued that the 11th

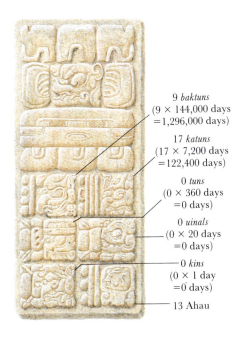

9 *baktuns*
(9 × 144,000 days
=1,296,000 days)

17 *katuns*
(17 × 7,200 days
=122,400 days)

0 *tuns*
(0 × 360 days
=0 days)

0 *uinals*
(0 × 20 days
=0 days)

0 *kins*
(0 × 1 day
=0 days)

13 Ahau

This portion of a Long Count or Initial Series date was translated by Sylvanus Morley from a stela at Quiriguá. The Maya date of 9.17.0.0.0 can be correlated with A.D. 771 in the Christian calendar.

baktun and 16th *katun* in the Long Count (conventionally written as 11.16.0.0.0) correlated with A.D. 1539. Another correlation proposed by anthropologist and art historian Herbert J. Spinden argued for an equation at the 12th *baktun* and 9th *katun* (12.9.0.0.0).

The Spinden correlation pushes back Maya hieroglyphic dates 260 years earlier in the Christian calendar than the Goodman-Martinez-Thompson correlation. For example, a hieroglyphic inscription that marks the beginning of the tenth *baktun* in the Maya calendar (a date of 10.0.0.0.0) would be correlated with a date in A.D. 830 using the Goodman-Martinez-Thompson correlation, but it would be read as a date in A.D. 570 using the Spinden correlation. Until quite recently no one was sure which correlation fit known archaeological sequences better, although the majority favored the G-M-T.

To investigate this problem, the University Museum of the University of Pennsylvania dated a series of wooden beams from Tikal that had good associations with hieroglyphic dates. The results of the carbon-14 assays run by the laboratory at the University Museum strongly supported the Goodman-Martinez-Thompson correlation. The Long Count would therefore be counting time from August 13, 3114 B.C. Although there continue to be some disagreements in the field, the argument has effectively ended. Thus, radiocarbon dating has enabled Maya archaeologists to build a tight chronological framework closely tied to the modern Christian calendar.

EXTERNAL INFLUENCES

Eric Thompson and his colleagues did not believe that the ancient Maya developed in total isolation from other cultures. However, while the traditional model did not ignore relations between the Maya and other groups, neither did it give them great weight. For example, when Morley talked about the earliest ceramics from Uaxactún or Northern Yucatán, he simply did not broach the question of where their sources might have lain. To Morley, Maya civilization arose as if by itself from the Southern Lowlands. Thompson, on the other hand, did consider where the first Maya settlers of the lowlands might have come from. He also recognized that the principal hallmarks of the Classic period—hieroglyphic writing, polychrome pottery, monumental art and architectural styles—had earlier predecessors in neighboring areas and therefore originated outside the lowlands. Nevertheless, there was very

Obsidian, which was fashioned into tools such as projectile points (left) or blades (right), was widely traded throughout the Maya Lowlands.

little discussion of how these traits reached the lowlands and what the exact nature of the external influences was. It was assumed, although never clearly argued why, that even though key aspects of lowland Maya culture had been derived from neighboring peoples, Classic Maya civilization developed by itself in a unique and separate fashion.

Traditional archaeologists recognized that during the Classic period the Maya were in contact with other peoples, such as the Teotihuacanos from the great urban center of Teotihuacán in the Basin of Mexico. But they did not think foreign contacts had significant impact on the Maya until after the collapse of Classic Maya civilization when, they argued, the Toltecs conquered Chichén Itzá. It was as if Maya scholars believed so strongly that Classic civilization was different and special that even if some cultural elements were derived from outside the lowlands, these external influences could not have had significant repercussions on the growth of Maya civilization. They assumed that the Maya elite picked and chose those traits they needed and were able to reject further influences.

The whole question of external contacts is obviously closely related to the question of long-distance trade. The traditional model recognized that elite items were traded regularly during the Classic period, but it left largely unexplored the mechanics of such trade and its implications for the religious, economic, social, and political organization of Maya civilization.

The putative isolation of the Maya in their jungle heartland has come under attack from many quarters in recent decades. External influences were much stronger and probably more significant than had previously been acknowledged. By Late Preclassic times there already was active trade with the Maya highlands. The similarities in ceramic designs and forms between the Maya lowlands and the Southern Highlands of Guatemala and El Salvador, particularly in the centuries just before and after the time of Christ, suggest that there were close contacts between the two areas. The highlands also traded obsidian, a volcanic glass used for sharp-edged tools, as well as jade, which was worn by the Maya elite in the form of bracelets, necklaces, and ear-plugs and was an important symbol of their rank and power.

There were connections, too, between the lowlands and other nearby regions, including the Northern Highlands of Guatemala and Chiapas and the Pacific Coast of Guatemala. The contacts are revealed by similarities in sculptural style, particularly when early Maya sculpture and hieroglyphic inscriptions from the third and fourth

Stela 2 from Izapa was first photographed by Matthew and Marion Sterling in 1941. Izapan sculptural art was an important precursor of Classic Maya art.

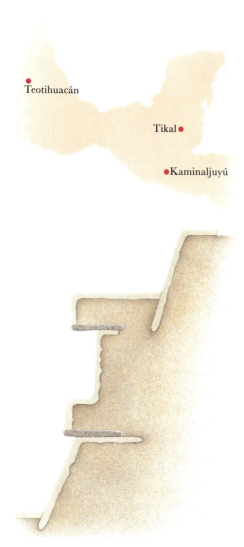

The *talud-tablero* architectural style consists of vertical framed panels directly above sloping basal aprons. It is a dominant feature at Teotihuacán, and its presence outside of the Valley of Mexico is a strong indicator of Teotihuacán influence.

centuries A.D. are compared to those of Northern Highland/Pacific Coastal sites such as Izapa, recently excavated by the New World Archaeological Foundation of Brigham Young University; Abaj Takalik, recently studied by the University of California at Berkeley; El Baúl; and the Southern Highland center of Kaminaljuyú, first excavated by the Carnegie Institution of Washington and more recently by Pennsylvania State University. The so-called Izapan style of the period immediately before and after the time of Christ links these and other sites. The monuments of Izapa show complex depictions of mythical and historical scenes; their elaborated garbed elite figures are reminiscent of the earlier Olmec style of the Gulf Coast lowlands and foreshadow the later Maya monumental style. Many scholars now believe that Maya hieroglyphic writing and monumental art derived from these sources, although they were developed much further and uniquely by the Maya.

Research at Tikal and other sites revealed that the Maya lowlands and Teotihuacán, along with other centers in Central Mexico, had a stronger relationship than previously suspected. Teotihuacán, located just northeast of modern-day Mexico City in a side valley off the Valley of Mexico, was the preeminent city of Central Mexico from about 150 B.C. to A.D. 750 and one of the greatest cities of Mesoamerica in Precolumbian times. A huge mapping project directed by the archaeologist Rene Millon of the University of Rochester and an excavation/restoration program by the Mexican government have provided a wealth of new data about this metropolis. At its height around A.D. 500, the city covered 20 square kilometers and supported a population of at least 125,000 and perhaps as many as 200,000. It was clearly one of the largest cities in the world at the time. It traded widely over Mesoamerica, but the nature of its "influence" outside of Central Mexico remains uncertain.

Whatever the exact nature of these influences, Teotihuacán was definitely in contact with Tikal. Moreover, continuing research at Tikal by Juan Pedro Laporte and his colleagues, supported by data from other sites in the lowlands, indicates that these contacts not only took place during Teotihuacán's heyday in Early Classic times but were in fact initiated in the Late Preclassic period. At Tikal, excavators have uncovered green obsidian from sources controlled by Teotihuacán, and they have found ceramics in Teotihuacán style, such as distinctive vases with tripod supports. Whether the vases were imports or local imitations is not always clear, although the former ap-

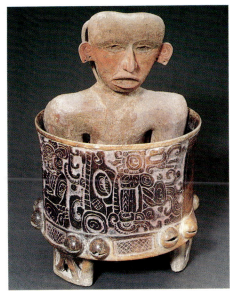

pears most often be the case. Architecture showing Teotihuacán influence, as well as Teotihuacán motifs in sculpture, also are found. One structure at Tikal is even built in the distinctive Teotihuacán *talud-tablero* style. Overall, the quantities of Teotihuacán or Teotihuacán-influenced items are not large but fairly widespread.

Studies of inscriptions and burials at Tikal have led scholars to hypothesize that contacts between Central Mexico and Teotihuacán may have been mediated through the center of Kaminaljuyú, located on the outskirts of modern-day Guatemala City. This city appears to have been conquered by Teotihuacán by the beginning of the Early Classic period. Investigators at Tikal, including Clemency Coggins, William Haviland, and Christopher Jones, have identified a ruler who ascended to the throne of Tikal in A.D. 378; the ruler is symbolized by a glyph labeled "Curl Nose." Coggins and others have argued that Curl Nose was an outsider who came to power by marrying into the local Jaguar Paw dynasty. Specifically, he married the daughter of the previous ruler. Coggins believes that Curl Nose may have come from Teotihuacán-dominated Kaminaljuyú. Curl Nose's son Stormy Sky

Left: The great city of Teotihuacán in Central Mexico was in contact with the lowland Maya from Late Preclassic through Early Classic times, although the nature of these contacts is a matter of much debate. *Right:* This decorated tripod bowl with a ceramic figurine inside was discovered at Becán; it dates to the end of the Early Classic period between A.D. 500 and 600. The hollow figurine contained ten smaller figurines and other materials. The vase is Classic Maya in style, whereas the figurine is clearly in the style of Teotihuacán. The art historian Flora Clancy argues that both bowl and figurine were probably manufactured in Becán with the presumed aim of juxtaposing the two different styles.

Stela 31 from Tikal dates to A.D. 445. It depicts the ruler Stormy Sky, the son of Curl Nose, and contains many Teotihuacán symbols.

came to power in A.D. 426. He is even more strongly associated with Teotihuacán symbols, including Teotihuacán warriors and Tlaloc, the Central Mexican rain god.

The nature of the contacts between the two cultures, whether economic, religious, military, or a combination, remains a matter of dispute. Even whether such contact was direct or indirect is an open question. Some archaeologists maintain that the Central Mexican traits at Tikal are an indication of a Teotihuacán embassy there.

Buildings, pottery, and other artifacts began to show fewer Teotihuacán traits throughout Mesoamerica in the seventh century A.D., and soon thereafter the great city's sphere of influence apparently contracted—perhaps as a result of internal problems in the city or its environs. It is my opinion that contacts between the lowlands and Central Mexico did not cease at this time. Rather, Maya cities, as well as other groups in the Gulf Coast region, may have begun to fill the vacuum created by Teotihuacán's decline. Goods, as well as ideas, probably continued to be interchanged.

Many scholars, myself included, are now convinced that the direction of influence was not always from Central Mexico to the Maya lowlands. The beautiful Late Classic painted murals at the Central Mexican site of Cacaxtla and Late Classic sculpture from Xochicalco to the southwest of the Valley of Mexico both show the definite presence of figures having typical Maya features and clothing.

Advances in archaeological chemistry, specifically in trace element analysis, have helped clarify particular questions of external influences and trade. Using the nondestructive technique of neutron activation on materials such as pottery, scientists can accurately measure the quantities of a wide variety of elements such as cadmium, chromium, or magnesium, which often appear in trace amounts. In this procedure, artifacts are subjected to nuclear bombardment, and as a result they emit rays, which are measured by special counters. Archaeologists can then group materials of similar makeup in order to see which ones originated from the same sources. In the case of certain materials like obsidian, samples from different sources have very distinctive trace element "signatures." Thus, it has been possible to link most of the highly prized obsidian tools found at Maya sites with specific obsidian sources, particularly two in the Southern Highlands of Guatemala: El Chayal and Jilotepeque.

By identifying sources of raw materials, archaeologists have been able to reconstruct trading routes from Preclassic through Postclassic times. Gone are the days when all the archaeologists could say was "these tools must have come from somewhere outside the lowlands!" Since obsidian is found in contexts as early as the Middle Preclassic (800–300 B.C.) and as late as the Spanish Conquest, archaeologists can also show how such routes developed and changed through time. These source identifications showed that long-distance trade and external relations played a significant role for the Maya well before the start of the Classic period.

A detailed neutron activation examination of a temperless pottery known as Fine Orange helped solidify the hypothesis discussed earlier that Seibal and Altar de Sacrificios were invaded during the ninth century A.D. The neutron activation study by the Brookhaven

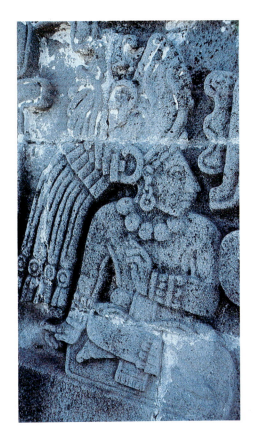

The Late Classic site of Xochicalco rose to prominence in the eighth century A.D. after the decline of Teotihuacán. As this carved Maya figure on one of its buildings indicates, Xochicalco was in contact with the lowland Maya world, although the nature of these contacts remains unknown.

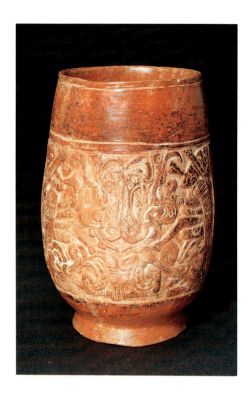

This Fine Orange vase, of the type known as Pabellon Modeled-carved, was found at Seibal in a Terminal Classic burial dating to the ninth century A.D. The design was made by impressing carved molds on the exterior of the vase. The figures and motifs on Pabellon vessels often resemble the non-Classic Maya figures on the Terminal Classic stelae at Seibal.

National Laboratory, the Peabody Museum of Harvard University, and Southern Illinois University showed that the Fine Orange pottery at both Seibal and Altar de Sacrificios, as well as other sites, had been made from closely related clays that could have come from zones along the greater Usumacinta River from its drainage into the Gulf of Mexico upriver to Altar de Sacrificios. Since the carved figures on the bowls and vases were very similar to figures depicting non-Classic Maya peoples on dated carved stelae from Seibal, it was possible to link the putative invaders with potential zones of origin in the Gulf Coast lowlands and the western border of the lowlands. Again, the significant role of outsiders in the development of Maya civilization was strongly supported by new technical analyses.

DIVERSITY WITHIN MAYA CULTURE

In large part because of the limited data available, but also because of its relatively monolithic view of Classic Maya civilization, the established model viewed the Classic period as a homogeneous entity both through time and space. Again, that is not to say that archaeologists were unaware of regional differences among sites or of changes through time. Rather, such differences were underplayed. This kind of thinking was in keeping with archaeology's general lack of interest in understanding variability prior to the 1960s.

In the past several decades, Maya archaeology has shared the advances in data recovery that the field as a whole has witnessed. Maya archaeologists today have available both newer and better kinds of information than their predecessors did. As would be expected, these richer data have revealed much greater variety in ancient lifeways. Scholars now recognize the changing complexity of the Classic Maya world. Each Southern Lowland center was not a carbon copy of the others, having access to similar lands and raw materials. Local resources differed, implying that ways of life varied and that regional exchange of goods, subsistence as well as elite, probably existed.

Careful screening of excavated materials is one simple new technique that has led to the recovery of new data of many kinds. In the past, as Maya archaeologists excavated, they simply threw the excavated dirt into piles after removing obvious artifacts like broken potsherds. Archaeologists now routinely throw the dirt onto one or more screens of various meshes in order to recover smaller fragments of

The screening of dirt from excavations on Cozumel. By using different-size meshes, researchers can uncover materials that might otherwise be missed by the naked eye, including small bits of stone or tiny fish bones.

material that might otherwise be overlooked as excavators shovel away dirt.

In the early 1970s on the island of Cozumel, for instance, my colleagues and I recovered over 20,000 pieces of animal bone from 77 different species through screening excavated materials. Analysis of the bones by Nancy Hamblin of the University of Arizona showed that more than 8,000 of them were the tiny bones of reef fishes. Many of the fish bones were from ancient domestic refuse deposits, suggesting that fish were an important source of food for the Precolumbian

Research at Colha by Tom Hester, Harry Shafer, and their colleagues has shown that the site was an important regional manufacturing center for chert tools. The excavation here revealed rich levels of chert waste debris produced during the chipping of tools.

Cozumeleños. In contrast, inland Maya (except those near rivers) did not eat fish but may occasionally have eaten wild game. Hamblin's studies of the bones of marine toads (*Bufo marinus*), often associated with burials, indicates that the toads may have been used during burial ceremonies for their hallucinogenic qualities. Thus, the efficient recovery of faunal materials through screening has allowed better understanding of diet as well as ritual.

Careful screening has also recovered pieces of lithic debitage—fragments of stone that are produced when stone tools are manufactured or reworked. Recovery of these fragments has been encouraged not only by better data retrieval techniques, but by changing perspectives on what kinds of archaeological materials are "significant" enough to collect. In the past, lithic chipping debris was unrecognized, ignored, or discarded, because it was deemed unimportant. With the recent recovery of such data, archaeologists have been able to locate manufacturing zones and to better understand the trade and distribution of tools.

An excellent example of Maya diversity can be found in the recent studies of lithic debitage at the site of Colha by the University of Texas at San Antonio. Fieldwork at Colha and other sites in northern Belize has shown that chert was mined at Colha and then manufactured into a variety of stone tools that were traded throughout the region. Studies at nearby Pulltrouser Swamp by Patricia McAnany of Boston University revealed that chert bifaces—axelike tools—were used to dig the earth around the artificial raised agricultural fields there; according to geological analysis, the chert had come from Colha. Moreover, careful study of the chert waste flakes at sites around Pulltrouser Swamp showed that the bifaces had not been manufactured there—the large quantities of debris at Colha would point to that center as the production site—but that the tools had been retouched or refinished as they wore down or were broken. The bifaces obviously were valuable enough (expensive to obtain?) to the people around Pulltrouser Swamp that when they were worn, damaged, or broken, they were not discarded but refinished and reused.

Chemical analyses of soils are another means that has enabled archaeologists to move away from unsupported traditional assumptions to more supportable statements about ancient Maya lifeways. Phosphate tests, for instance, can show where food was grown. A successful application of this technique occurred during our recent research at the site of Sayil. Nicholas Dunning of the University of Min-

nesota, Thomas Killion of Boston University, Gair Tourtellot of Dumbarton Oaks, and I have been able to hypothesize that parts of large cleared areas near residential platforms—what are often called "plazas"—were used as kitchen gardens by the families living in the adjacent houses. This kind of information can then be used in larger hypotheses about changing demographic patterns and local agricultural carrying capacities.

Maya civilization continued to change throughout the Classic period. Population increased at many established centers, although not always steadily. The population became increasingly nucleated, or concentrated in the centers of cities. Many new centers were established, particularly in the Late Classic, as the Maya filled in much of the previously uninhabited or lightly occupied parts of the lowlands. Moreover, toward the end of the Late Classic it became increasingly difficult to feed and organize the large populations.

There are also indications of growing social stratification and lessening social mobility. Analyses of burials and other studies have

A Maya farmer is turning over soil and pulling out weeds with a chert biface axe, while another farmer sharpens his biface by chipping the end.

107

The lid over the sarcophagus of Pacal, the
great ruler of Palenque, is a marvelous example of the complexity and beauty of Maya
monumental sculpture. Pacal's elaborate tomb
is also an example of the growing wealth and
power of the ruling elite during Late Classic
times.

revealed that the elite became more powerful and wealthy than ever before. For example, a study by William Rathje of the University of Arizona shows that through time there are fewer wealthy burials in locations well away from the centers of sites. Heredity seemed to become more important, as children were buried with many grave goods that they could not have earned through their own work.

Studies of architecture indicate that the bureaucracy appeared to be growing in size and importance. The number of "palaces" compared to temples rises throughout the Classic (if the contention is accepted that at least some of the "palaces" were used for public activities by elite functionaries). Proskouriakoff's drawings of Structure A-V at Uaxactún, reproduced on page 46, show one example of a complex that had been dominated by three temples early in Classic times. But a few centuries later the temples were all but masked by long, low "palaces." Studies of newly mapped centers show that the spatial organization of site cores changed during the Classic, too, as public access to sacred space seemed to decrease through time.

Finally, a host of data suggests that as the population grew and cities became larger, there was growing pressure on the agricultural systems supporting these centers. On the one hand, some data point to an expansion of the number of non-food producers during Late Classic times, while on the other, cores drilled in the bottom of Southern Lowland lakes reveal increased soil erosion and salinization that perhaps were caused by overuse of the soil. Because the erosion occurred just prior to the Classic demise in the Southern Lowlands, it may indicate that overpopulation and agricultural pressures were key factors in that collapse. In response to such pressure, the Maya may well have widened their emphasis on intensive agricultural techniques like terracing or reclamation. Although such techniques were first used earlier, they become much more important toward the end of the Classic period. Pollen collected in the Copán Valley by David Rue indicate that by the end of the Late Classic period, most trees in the valley had been cut down, presumably to make room for agricultural production.

Although pollen analyses and other new techniques have given archaeologists fresh insights upon which to build new interpretations of the Maya, the revolutionary new views of Maya civilization have sprung largely from changes in thinking and perspective within the discipline of archaeology as a whole and among Mayanists in particular. These intellectual changes, in turn, led to the application of new methods such as settlement pattern studies.

4

NEW

VIEWS

OF

THE

PRECLASSIC

AND

POSTCLASSIC

PERIODS

The Arch (foreground) and the Mirador
(background) at Labná in the Puuc region of
the Northern Lowlands.

When traditional archaeologists bothered to look at all at Maya civilization before and after the Classic period, it was with scorn or condescension. They saw the Preclassic Maya as primitive villagers and the Postclassic Maya as third-rate imitators of their ancestors. You won't be surprised to learn that modern archaeologists have set out to challenge this view, and that they have uncovered evidence showing the early Maya to be more precocious and the later Maya more sophisticated than anyone had suspected. In fact, archaeologists are even questioning the dating of the established periods of ancient Maya development. They now suggest that many of the impressive Classic Maya traits were actually present at least several centuries earlier in the Late Preclassic, while most familiar features of the Late Classic south reappear in the Early Postclassic north. From a modern point of view, the "Classic" heyday of the Maya arguably lasted from 300 B.C. to A.D. 1250 and the rise of Mayapán.

THE BEGINNINGS OF MAYA CIVILIZATION

Until a few years ago, archaeologists believed that civilization, or complex society, emerged in the Maya lowlands around the end of the third century A.D., which marked the beginning of the Classic period. At about this time surfaced many of the exceptional characteristics of Classic civilization: the Maya carved their first hieroglyphs on stone monuments, they began to manufacture polychrome ceramics with lovely complex designs, and they constructed the monumental stone architecture of the first large ceremonial centers. Although it became clear over the years that the hieroglyphs, polychrome pottery, and monumental architecture did not appear simultaneously and that they had evolved from earlier precursors, it was nevertheless thought that they attained recognizable form about A.D. 300. And so that date could still be used as the starting point for Classic civilization in the Maya lowlands.

The large-scale Preclassic architecture found at Tikal put the first chink in the traditional view of the rise of Maya civilization. By the end of the 1970s, a host of other important field projects in both the Southern and Northern lowlands were challenging the old view. These projects clearly showed that complex urban centers began to develop at least as far back as 300 B.C. Particularly important excavations were undertaken in the north at Dzibilchaltún (directed by E. Wyllys An-

drews IV of the Middle American Research Institute, Tulane University, in the 1950s and 1960s) and, later, Komchén (directed by E. Wyllys Andrews V of the same institution in the early 1980s), and in the south at El Mirador (particularly the project directed by Ray Matheny of Brigham Young University in the late 1970s and early 1980s), Cerros (directed by David Freidel and Robin Robertson of Southern Methodist University from 1974 to 1981), Lamanai (directed by David Pendergast of the Royal Ontario Museum in the 1970s and 1980s), and Cuello (directed by Norman Hammond in the 1970s and 1980s).

Although archaeologists have learned a great deal about the period from 300 B.C. to A.D. 300, the years from the first Maya settlement of the lowlands to 300 B.C. remain opaque in comparison. One principal reason for this lacuna in archaeological understanding is purely practical: because of the Maya penchant for building right on top of earlier structures, much of the Middle Preclassic material lies below centuries of building and rebuilding. It can be difficult, time-consum-

Ignored and mostly untouched by the Classic Maya, the site of Komchén offers archaeologists the opportunity to explore Preclassic development in the Northern Lowlands without having to dig through layers of overburden. E. Wyllys Andrews V and his colleagues have found that an area in excess of 2 square kilometers was heavily populated during Preclassic times. Structure 500, a portion of which is shown here, consisted in the Middle Preclassic of a large platform with a small temple-pyramid. The remains above come from the enlarged temple constructed in the Late Preclassic.

Archaeologists often find it difficult to uncover Middle Preclassic material because of the ancient Maya habit of building repeatedly on the same site. For example, in this cross section of the North Acropolis at Tikal, the Middle Preclassic pit lies below many meters of later construction.

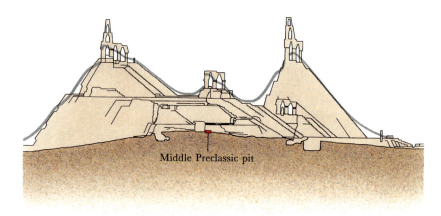

Middle Preclassic pit

Preclassic figurines, such as this Middle Preclassic example from Altar de Sacrificios, were handmade, unlike Classic figurines, which usually were produced by molds. The Middle Preclassic figurines also tend to be cruder in style than later ones.

ing, and extremely expensive to carefully strip off all the overburden to reveal large areas of Middle Preclassic occupation. Most of the little scholars know about this period comes from the bottom of deep pits and trenches, where they usually unearth nothing but potsherds and pieces of flint and obsidian from ambiguous settings. Because archaeologists often look at the Middle Preclassic level from the bottom of a 2-by-2-meter pit, they usually have little idea of what type of structure or environment the materials come from. Middle Preclassic ceramics also are found in the mixed architectural fills of later buildings; unfortunately, having been removed from their original surroundings, these ceramics also tell us little about Middle Preclassic lifeways.

What little archaeologists do know about this early period suggests that while the lowlands appear to have been sporadically occupied for many millennia by groups of hunters and gatherers, the Maya first settled in the lowlands by 800 B.C. at the latest and probably as early as 1000 to 1200 B.C. E. Wyllys Andrews V has convincingly argued that groups of farmers first moved into the Southern Lowlands from two separate areas. One group was a Maya-speaking people from the highlands of Northern Guatemala who settled in the northeast zone of the Southern Lowlands at sites such as Cuello. The other was a non-Maya-speaking group from the highlands of Chiapas who settled in the Pasión River valley at sites like Altar de Sacrificios and Seibal. These groups lived in small villages and grew maize as their principal subsistence crop, as we know, for example, by the findings of maize pollen and grinding stones at Cuello. By 600 B.C., the Maya had begun to spread into unsettled parts of the lowlands. Whether they mixed with the non-Maya group in the Pasión River valley or pushed the non-Maya to the west remains unclear. Even from these early times, the Maya imported materials such as obsidian from the highlands.

Between 600 and 300 B.C., the population of the lowland Maya burgeoned. As villages grew in size, pioneer groups split off to set up new villages. The first examples of public architecture—platforms with no clear domestic functions—probably date to this time. It has been hypothesized that the platforms served a religious purpose. If so, they point to the growing importance of the priesthood, who acted as mediators between the peasants and the deities, such as the rain god, that could influence the health of crops. The rising populations could have fed the priests and provided the labor to build public structures.

Growth certainly continued and may even have quickened in the last centuries of the first millennium B.C. The Maya of the Late Preclassic period from 300 B.C. to A.D. 300 had the ability to mobilize large numbers of people to build huge temples and to feed those large numbers. They created complicated iconographic motifs, participated in far-flung trading networks, and exploited their organizational "know-how" to maintain swelling urban centers.

The growing importance of trade is reflected in the rise of Cerros in northern Belize. Before the time of Christ, this center was a flourishing trading port, and it probably owes its development to its strategic location on a protected bay near the mouth of the New River, which flows from the interior of Belize. Archaeologists have found evidence of an ancient dock at Cerros. Ceramic analyses indicate that Cerros was in close contact with other lowland centers, as do motifs on large stucco masks decorating pyramids. Cerros may have acted as a way station for raw materials such as obsidian, jade, and other hard stone coming from the highlands and for cotton and cacao, as well as finished elite materials like finely worked jade, going from the northeastern corner of the Southern Lowlands to other zones. Decorated ceramics also may have been traded from the Southern Highlands to the lowlands.

The sheer monumentality and extent of buildings such as Structure 4C-54 (the Lost World Pyramid) at Tikal, N10-43 at Lamanai, and especially the Tigre complex at El Mirador are impressive examples of the scale that the Late Preclassic Maya elite worked in. The main pyramid in the Tigre complex, for example, towers 55 meters over the jungle floor and may be unmatched in height by any other construction during the Late Preclassic, except for the Danta complex at the same site which was built on a natural rise. The Tikal pyramid

The symbolic stucco masks on Structure 5C-2nd at Cerros are evidence that Late Preclassic architecture was much more substantial and sophisticated than previously thought.

is 20 meters in height and 80 meters to a side at its base, while the Lamanai building rose 33 meters in height. Just as in Classic times, these buildings were often part of large complexes built around plazas, and they were constructed of finely cut limestone blocks covered by plaster. However, despite their resemblance to Classic buildings, they do not yet make use of corbelled vaults. Some of these buildings had elaborate stucco masks on the exterior walls that flanked stairways. These masks mark the beginning of the Maya high art style, and show complex religious symbols. On the other hand, full-scale hieroglyphic writing was not in evidence throughout much of the Late Preclassic period. Thus one of the traditional markers of civilization in the lowlands was apparently not critical to the rise of Classic culture.

Payson Sheets of the University of Colorado has argued that lava flows from a major volcanic eruption devastated portions of the Southern Highlands during the Late Preclassic, destroying agricultural fields. This catastrophe, Sheets suggests, may have set off a large migration to the lowlands that would have further swelled lowland population. Although this hypothesis is very controversial, it is possible that a rapidly climbing population spurred the rise of advanced civilization. By Late Preclassic times, competition for land, people, and resources may have led to warfare between cities. For example, Webster has argued that the moat and parapet at Becán may well date to this

period. How critical such conflicts were in the formation of complex cities is obviously a matter of debate, although I believe they were a crucial factor. Conflict would have forced people to group together for security. The elite in the centers may have encouraged migration to the cities in order to obtain larger labor and military forces. In turn, large cities would require greater planning and organization in order to provide and distribute food to the urban laborers and to form and equip a militia, as well as to build defensive structures.

Whatever the seeds that led to its rise, Maya civilization flowered in the Southern Lowlands for a number of centuries—until inexplicably the great cities began to disappear.

The immense Late Preclassic Structure N10-43 from Lamanai towered 33 meters above the plaza floor. As on the temple from Cerros, large stucco masks depicting Maya deities flank the lower stairs.

THE COLLAPSE IN THE SOUTH

Around A.D. 800, many cities in the Southern Lowlands went into disastrous declines. Monumental architecture ceased to be constructed, carved stelae were no longer erected, and the ceremonial centers of these cities were virtually abandoned. In recent years, settlement surveys have showed that the Maya deserted many suburban and rural areas around the cities, too. Judging from the obvious indicators, Classic civilization in the Southern Lowlands came to an abrupt halt.

Why did Classic Maya civilization in the Southern Lowlands decline in the ninth century A.D.? This question has tantalized archaeologists and the general public alike. Numerous hypotheses have been put forward to explain this historical phenomenon—it seems that there have been as many hypotheses as there have been Maya archaeologists!—but the roots of the "collapse" have remained controversial. As might be expected, as archaeologists' views of the ancient Maya have changed, so have their explanations of the sudden decline.

Although earlier archaeologists never reached a consensus, most of the older views of the collapse emphasized single factors, many of them catastrophic in nature. Earthquakes, hurricanes, climatic changes, disease, insect pests, warfare, soil exhaustion, and peasant revolts were all proffered at one time or another as possible solutions to the "mystery" or the collapse. Exceptions were raised to all of these single-factor explanations, however, and no one proposed cause of collapse gained widespread acceptance.

This confusion prevailed until the early 1970s, when the new perspectives on Classic civilization stimulated a rethinking of the reasons for its death. A lightning rod for these new ideas was a week-long seminar held at the School of American Research in Santa Fe, New Mexico, in 1970. After reexamining the whole question of the collapse in light of the advances of the 1960s, eleven scholars, including myself, came up with a revisionist view of the end of Classic civilization. The seminar participants agreed that the collapse could not be considered as an isolated event. In order to understand the collapse, we argued, archaeologists had to understand the changing nature of Maya civilization prior to the collapse. Classic civilization in turn had to be viewed in the wider context of cultural processes taking place elsewhere in Mesoamerica, and archaeologists also needed to appreciate the ecological underpinnings of Maya civilization.

The seminar participants agreed that the problem was not only what caused the collapse in the Southern Lowlands, but why the region never recovered. Although collapsed civilizations are commonplace throughout history, they often recover at least to some extent. Occasionally, the renewed civilization is even more spectacular than the one before, although in other instances it is a pale reflection of the earlier culture. Thus, one of the most intriguing and eye-catching aspects of the Classic Maya collapse has been the complete lack of recovery in the Southern Lowlands up to the present day. Even now much of the region is sparsely populated.

Scholars at the seminar noted that by the end of the eighth century, Classic Maya society was under great internal and external stress. Population was growing significantly and social stratification was intensifying. The elite were becoming wealthier, more powerful, and more numerous, and they were expanding the bureaucracy, which—from "palace offices"—presumably oversaw the feeding and housing of the urban populations. On the other hand, the bulk of the Maya were becoming less privileged, as shown, for example, by their decreasing access to sacred space. Because the proportion of the populace devoted to producing food rapidly decreased, the agricultural system had trouble supplying enough for everyone to eat. Analysis of skeletons shows some malnutrition and possibly an increase in disease. As a consequence of food shortages, competition between centers increased, and cities launched more raids against their rivals for control of people and land. Management problems also grew heavier for the elite, as they had to increase food production and distribution, find more labor and materials for new construction, and protect the expanding cities.

During the Late Classic, the ruling elite expended some of their huge wealth on elaborate burials, such as the entombment of Palenque's great ruler Pacal. Pacal's body was bedecked with jewelry and a beautiful jade mosaic death mask and then placed in an elaborately carved sarcophagus (see page 108) set into a specially prepared chamber.

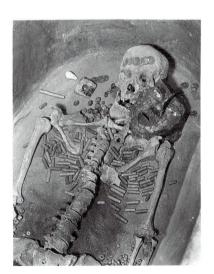

At the same time that internal strains were reaching a head, external pressures emerged, particularly along the western frontier of the Southern Lowlands. Non-Classic Maya peoples from the Gulf Coast lowlands attacked the frontier, possibly cutting off trade routes. One example of their incursions was the conquest of Seibal and Altar de Sacrificios discussed in the last chapter. These two sites may in turn have been used as bases for raids on other lowland centers.

The seminar participants suggested that the Classic Maya rulers were aware of both kinds of stress and attempted to respond. They founded new centers, reclaimed ever more swampland, and initiated massive building projects. The grand new structures may have been intended to glorify the gods and thereby decrease the strains, but instead they took even more workers away from agriculture, since new laborers were needed to quarry limestone, cut it, transport it, and carve it. The net effect was to make the Maya more vulnerable to disasters that might normally not have been severe, although scholars could not pinpoint what kind of disaster was the exact trigger for rapid decline. Nevertheless, they were able to identify a series of factors, all of which were closely related ("systemically reinforcing" in modern parlance).

Scholars at the seminar also maintained that widespread land clearance as well as attempts to intensify agricultural production led to severe soil depletion. The degradation of the environment was one of the reasons, it was contended, that the Southern Lowlands did not recover after the ninth-century collapse. Ecological studies have since indicated that there was indeed heavy erosion at the time of the collapse and that much of the forest cover had been eliminated. In fact, research since the early 1970s has reinforced many of the hypotheses advanced at the seminar.

The seminar concluded that in response to the threatened destruction of their culture, the Maya chose solutions that were not only futile but damaging. Their response had been determined by the cultural trends during the Classic period and by the nature of Classic Maya sociopolitical organization and ideology. In effect, without significant technological changes, the Southern Lowland environment could not support a civilization as complex as the eighth-century Maya, and the needed technology did not arise.

New studies in the Northern Lowlands have resolved one of the questions that divided Thompson and Morley: Did the northern centers arise after or during the southern collapse? We now know that the

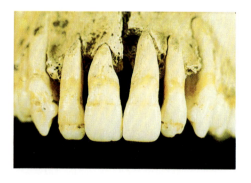

Research by Frank and Julie Saul indicates that the horizontal markings on these teeth are lesions commonly found among the ancient Maya. The teeth belonged to a young adult male from Seibal who lived in the ninth century A.D. His lesions may have been caused by malnutrition between ages three and four, when he would no longer have been receiving protein from his mother's milk.

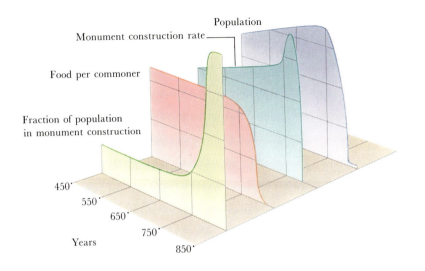

Population

Monument construction rate

Food per commoner

Fraction of population
in monument construction

450
550
650
750
Years
850

The explanation for the Classic collapse that was developed by the School of American Research seminar participants was converted into a mathematical simulation model by Dorothy Hosler, Dale Runge, and myself. This computer simulation showed that increasing population, a resulting shortage of food, and burgeoning construction, along with a host of other factors, *could have* caused the collapse.

rise of great Puuc region sites such as Uxmal, Kabah, Sayil, and Labná, the florescence of Chichén Itzá, and the development of the east coast of the Yucatán Peninsula all occurred at the same time as the decline in the south. Moreover, there were strong similarities between the Southern and Northern Lowland cities, in agricultural practices, city planning, architecture, tools, hieroglyphic writing, and religion. In other words, Classic Maya civilization did not collapse: instead, its population and center of political-economic power shifted from south to north. As the anthropologist Charles Erasmus of the University of California at Santa Barbara has noted, there was an "upward" collapse both culturally to a more politically complex Maya society and geographically to the crowded Puuc region and Chichén Itzá.

Some southern centers, such as Lamanai and Nohmul in Belize, remained robust and well-populated throughout the ninth century. Those cities in the Southern Lowlands that did not collapse appear to have been located near waterborne trade routes or in zones where "cash" crops such as cacao or cotton could have been produced. These recent findings point to another possible reason for the lack of recovery in the south. Centers nearby the Maya lowlands and in the Mexican highlands may have been demanding resources, goods, or crops that

During the Terminal Classic period, Maya civilization shifted from the Southern to the Northern Lowlands. However, some Southern Lowland cities with favorable locations continued to flourish, most notably in northern Belize, the lakes region to the south of Tikal *(shaded)*, and areas along the western and southern borders.

much of the Southern Lowlands could not produce. This merchandise may have been transported in bulk by water routes that bypassed much of the landlocked south. Given the severe soil erosion in the Southern Lowlands, there was no economic motivation to invest heavily in the area and bring it back to its former glory. And so the south was passed over in favor of the north and those few southern cities and regions having the right soil, climate, and location.

FLORESCENCE IN THE NORTH

A host of new data about Maya settlement, epigraphy, architecture, and trade has filled in important, long-standing gaps in the story of the relatively neglected north. It now appears that Classic civilization had a final flowering in the Northern Lowlands from A.D. 800 to 1000 (what is now called the Terminal Classic period). This flourishing period may have lasted perhaps as late as 1200, when Chichén Itzá apparently went into decline. Admittedly, there are some stylistic differences in architecture and ceramics compared to the Classic period, such as the introduction of veneer masonry, the use of facades decorated with stone mosaic designs, the growing employment of columns in place of doors and vaults to open up rooms, and the demise of polychrome painting on ceramics in favor of much simpler decorations. Before the end of Terminal Classic times, the carving of hieroglyphic inscriptions on monuments had completely died out. Still, as noted earlier, the overall similarities in site layout, architecture, religion, and probably sociopolitical organization far outweigh the differences. That is to say, Uxmal is as "Classic" as Palenque.

Terminal Classic civilization centered in the Puuc region, the only hilly zone in northern Yucatán, and in Chichén Itzá. The Puuc region has some of the best soils in the area and therefore great agricultural potential. However, sources of water are scarce. Although rainfall can be heavy during the rainy season from about May through January,

The great Puuc site of Uxmal thrived during the Terminal Classic period. Part of the architectural core is shown here, including the House of the Turtles, left foreground; the ball court, near center; the Nunnery quadrangle, far center; and the Temple of the Magician, right.

The Puuc architectural style featured elaborate stone mosaics that had both geometric and naturalistic designs. Many of the motifs were repeated, and the mosaic parts were apparently mass produced. This example is a repetitive rain god design from the site of Kabah.

This ancient collapsed *chultun* at Sayil gives a clear view of the cistern in cross section, revealing its restricted opening and plastered chamber.

the rainwater quickly percolates through the limestone surface. There are no *cenotes* or natural wells, as there are in other parts of the Northern Lowlands. Thus, in order to exploit the rich soils, the Maya had to put in place a water capture system. Although the region had been sporadically occupied before the Terminal Classic period—at sites like Oxkintok—it wasn't until the eighth century that the Maya achieved the organization and leadership, as well as the technical know-how, to build large numbers of *chultunes* (underground cisterns) that collected water during the rainy season for use during the dry season.

The population of the Puuc region built up rapidly around A.D. 800—just the time that many Southern Lowland cities were disappearing. However, there are no strong indications that the population explosion in the Puuc was fed by migrations from the Southern Lowlands. Nevertheless, the new Puuc populations may have come in part from the Chenes region just to the south of the Puuc, which in turn might have been under pressure from areas, such as the Rio Bec region, still farther south.

An elaborate façade in the Chenes architectural style, which some scholars see as a precursor to the Puuc style.

The *sacbe* connecting Uxmal and Kabah terminates at Kabah in a platform supporting a freestanding arch with corbeled vaulting.

Many of the Puuc cities stood close together—for example, Kabah lies about 7 kilometers to the north of Sayil, while Labná is about 5 kilometers to the east. That and the presence of many smaller centers and settlements between the cities, as well as the presence of *sacbes* (paved roads or causeways lined with stones) including one linking Uxmal and Kabah, have led scholars to suppose that there must have been closer political cooperation among the Puuc cities than had previously existed in the lowlands. Cooperation among centers seems even more likely in light of the absence of many of the common indicators of warfare and conflict.

The reasons why the Puuc centers disappeared after only two centuries remain unknown. However, according to the settlement study at Sayil, the population of the urban zone and its sustaining area had reached the estimated carrying capacity of its environment by the end of the ninth century. Nevertheless, whether soil erosion or lack of water or competition with Chichén Itzá led to the fall of the Puuc sites is still cause for speculation. Answers must wait for more intensive studies, like the Sayil research, in the Puuc zone.

CHICHÉN ITZÁ

Recent research at Chichén Itzá, along with reanalyses of older data, indicates that there was a significant overlap in the occupations of the Puuc sites and Chichén Itzá, rather than the Puuc–Chichén Itzá sequence that some archaeologists traditionally argued for. The extent of this overlap is currently a matter of some debate, although most archaeologists would agree that the two centers were thriving together for at least a while. Unfortunately, the economic and political relationships between the Puuc region cities and Chichén Itzá still remain unclear.

Archaeologists are now rethinking the conventional division of the remains at Chichén Itzá into an earlier Maya phase and a later Toltec one, which had been one of the components of the argument that Chichén Itzá was conquered by the Toltecs from Central Mexico sometime in the tenth century A.D. Because not much excavation has been carried out at Chichén Itzá, outside of work related to restoration, the arguments for a Toltec conquest have generally relied on

Below: A *chac-mool* statue sits in front of the Temple of the Warriors in the so-called new section of Chichén Itzá. The similarity of this and other structures with buildings at the Central Mexican site of Tula, capital of the Toltecs, led many scholars to believe that Chichén Itzá was conquered by the Toltecs, a view now being challenged. In fact, many archaeologists now argue that these structures were built by Maya peoples who were directly or indirectly in contact, probably through trade, with Central Mexico. *Left* (*below*): The Nunnery (left) and the Church in "Old Chichén" were built in the Maya style typical of the Terminal Classic period in the Northern Lowlands. Many scholars now find little evidence that these structures were built much earlier than the supposed "Toltec" ones.

Toltec styles found in surface materials. Buildings with Central Mexican forms, figures, and symbols appeared to be in a separate area ("New Chichén") from the Maya buildings ("Old Chichén"). The new research indicates that this supposed separation was more apparent than real, and that it is not supported by stratigraphic excavations.

Some have suggested that many of the so-called Toltec attributes had either been present in the Maya area well before the tenth century or were not Toltec at all. Moreover, it now appears that the interaction between the Northern Maya Lowlands and Central Mexico was not just one-way, but that the Maya significantly influenced Mexican peoples, as seen, for instance, at the recently discovered murals at Cacaxtla, which show dignitaries in Maya costume. Thus, while the Northern Lowlands were in contact with Central Mexico and Oaxaca, it is not clear how direct such contacts were—they might have been mediated by merchants from the Gulf Coast lowlands—nor what their exact nature was. At the moment, the case for conquest is not relatively strong.

Anthony Andrews of the University of South Florida and his colleagues have located a small island just off the north coast, Isla Cerritos, that may have served as Chichén Itzá's port and its economic link to far-flung areas, particularly Central Mexico. Quantities of green obsidian from a Central Mexican source, for example, have been discovered in excavations on the island. The Isla Cerritos research adds weight to arguments advanced by Andrews and Fernando Robles Castellanos of the National Institute of Anthropology and History in Mexico that Chichén Itzá was the capital of a state that controlled much of the central portion of the Northern Lowlands. Their examination of the spatial distribution of Chichén Itzá–influenced ceramics and architecture leads them to a working hypothesis that this expanding state may have come into conflict with another political entity on the east coast of the peninsula, which had the large city of Cobá as its center.

Chichén Itzá was a religious center of widespread importance. Even after its demise by the thirteenth century, it remained one of the great pilgrimage centers in the Maya world, along with the shrine of Ix Chel, the Maya goddess of the moon and childbirth, on the Island of Cozumel and the huge pyramid at Izamal to the northeast of Chichén Itzá. Pilgrims visited Chichén Itzá well into the sixteenth century, particularly to view rituals at the Sacred Well (*Cenote* of Sacrifice).

The ninth-century murals at the Central Mexican site of Cacaxtla show clear Maya influences, such as these dignitaries in Maya costume.

The Sacred *Cenote* at Chichén Itzá is a natural well that was a focus of religious ceremonies for many centuries. Dredgings of the well have uncovered numerous religious offerings, including many made from perishable materials, which have been preserved in silt.

Chichén Itzá continued to be an important center perhaps as late as A.D. 1200 or 1250, although these dates are uncertain, as are the reasons for the city's decline. Because a wide-scale, extensive settlement pattern study is lacking, archaeologists don't so much as have a clue to Chichén Itzá's population at its height! The need for such a study at Chichén Itzá, along with intensive excavations, is pressing, and it is my hope that recent small-scale research at the site will be followed by the kinds of major projects this great center deserves.

The heyday of Chichén Itzá spans both the Terminal Classic and Early Postclassic periods in current Maya chronology. Some scholars, myself included, would now place the boundary between the Terminal Classic and Postclassic periods at the time of Chichén Itzá's decline. For us, with the fall of Chichén Itzá the Classical period comes to a close. Clearly, the older chronological terms and periods need a major overhaul in the coming years.

The first column of this chart depicts the traditional chronological scheme for the development of ancient Maya civilization. The second shows my current view of the significant breaks in lowland Maya chronology. The pottery illustrated in the chart comes from the three major periods. The Preclassic and Classic pieces are from Uaxactún, and the Postclassic is from Mayapán.

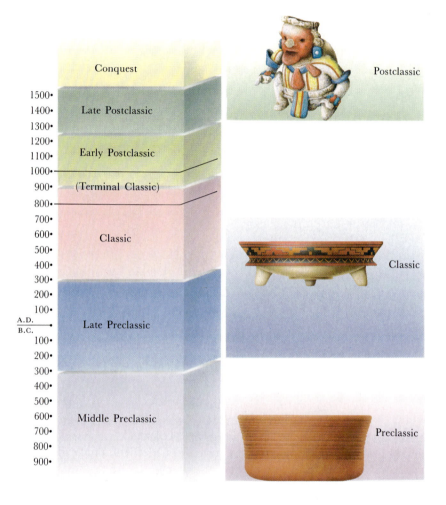

Conquest

1500•
1400• Late Postclassic
1300•
1200•
1100• Early Postclassic
1000•
900• (Terminal Classic)
800•
700•
600•
500• Classic
400•
300•
200•
100•
A.D.
B.C.
100• Late Preclassic
200•
300•
400•
500•
600• Middle Preclassic
700•
800•
900•

Postclassic

Classic

Preclassic

THE "DECADENT" PERIOD

The late Postclassic or Decadent period (A.D. 1250–1520) is usually identified with two sites: Mayapán and Tulum. Both sites were principally explored prior to 1960, at a time when archaeologists tended to deride their strikingly different, "inferior" culture. Although scholars have relatively little new data to consider, with the exception of art historian Arthur Miller's important new studies of the Tulum murals, some are looking at earlier knowledge with new eyes.

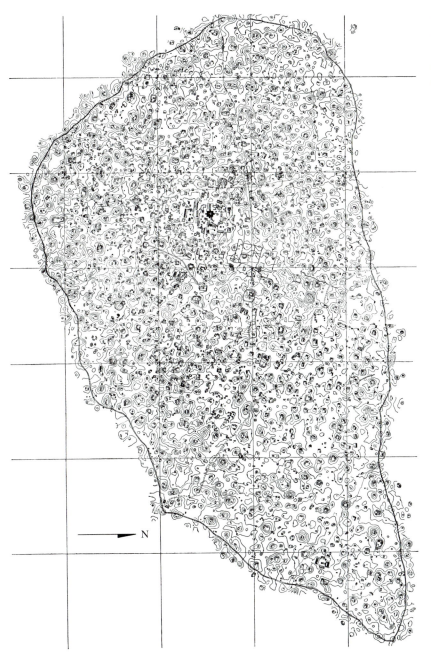

N

Mayapán was a densely populated urban center surrounded by a wall, traits clearly shown on this map prepared by M. R. Jones for the Carnegic Institute of Washington. Its population of 12,000 occupied an area of only 4 square kilometers.

Mayapán succeeded Chichén Itzá as the major center in northern Yucatán. From 1250 to 1450, it kept together by force a confederacy encompassing much of the Northern Lowlands. In contrast to the leisurely, spread-out cities of an earlier time, both Mayapán and the much smaller center Tulum were compactly laid out between walls. Tulum was dramatically situated on a cliff, protected by the sea on one side and its walls on another. The walled center and other defensive measures suggest that the Late Postclassic period was a time of frequent warfare and raiding.

The traditional archaeology scoffed at the "tacky," mass-produced ceramics unearthed at these sites, but mass production is a technique requiring sophisticated planning, and, as we know, it makes more goods available to the middle and lower classes. Although the traditional archaeologists blamed the downfall of religion for the supposed deterioration of Maya culture, in fact religion remained very important. But it was not as centralized as before; the Late Postclassic Maya generally worshipped at family shrines rather than at large central temples. The elaborate, mass-produced incense burners of the day

The Castillo at the center of Mayapán appears as the large black square on the map on the preceding page. This structure is a smaller copy of the Castillo at Chichén Itzá, and is the only large temple-pyramid at this site.

are also evidence that the practice of religion was in the hands of the lowly individual. The hints we see in Mayapán and Tulum of a society less dominated by its traditional elite become bolder in my own studies of the Island of Cozumel.

Research directed by William Rathje and myself on Cozumel focused on trade during this period. We knew from sixteenth-century Spanish documents that Cozumel had been a trading center; we wanted to see how such a trading center functioned in Postclassic times. Our fieldwork on Cozumel allowed us to argue that although the art and architecture of the Late Postclassic certainly had declined from the high aesthetic standards of the Classic period, the culture as a whole was not necessarily "decadent." Surveys and excavation that we undertook in 1972 and 1973 indicated that the entire island had more than 30 sites and was densely populated. Cozumel was highly organized, with a central capital (San Gervasio), a system of roads, and areas set aside for specialized functions such as warehousing. The standard of living for the population as a whole seemed to have risen from earlier times, as we found goods formerly reserved for the elite in

The remains of several Late Postclassic shrines lie on this platform at the site of Agu-ada Grande on the Island of Cozumel.

The Island of Cozumel off the east coast of the Yucatán Peninsula flourished from Terminal Classic times, through its heyday in the Late Postclassic period, and up until the Spanish Conquest. More than thirty sites have been found on the island, the largest being San Gervasio. Because of Cozumel's flat landscape, the inhabitants built many large centers inland for protection against raids. Causeways linked inland centers to northern lagoons, where canoes carrying goods for long-distance trade could be unloaded.

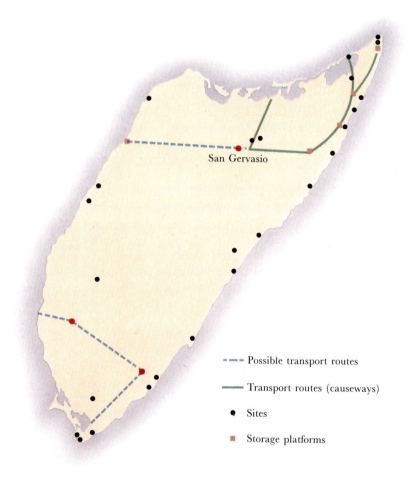

San Gervasio

- - - - Possible transport routes

——— Transport routes (causeways)

● Sites

■ Storage platforms

all kinds of settings. Cozumel participated in complex trading systems that put the island in touch with far-flung regions.

Moreover, the ethos of the time appears to have changed. The more mercantile-oriented elite were less interested in public displays of wealth and power, especially in large religious edifices, and more concerned with keeping their wealth fluid. Even in their ceremonial

offerings—placed under a new shrine, for example—they followed tradition by including valuable exotic items like greenstone axes, but they often made an offering of broken axes, presumably to keep the whole ones in circulation. Religion, while apparently as important as ever, had become more decentralized and less politically powerful, and the religious elite were less able than before to mobilize large labor forces. Our research on Cozumel clearly showed that while the culture of the Postclassic was changing it was not necessarily declining.

Our research at Cozumel is but one example from many of the projects examining previously neglected time periods, the Preclassic and Postclassic, and formerly ignored regions, particularly in the Northern Lowlands. These projects have shown that Maya civilization began many centuries before the traditional start of the Classic period. Moreover, it did not slide downhill after its collapse in the Southern Lowlands around A.D. 800. Instead, it continued to flourish in the Northern Lowlands for several centuries until the fall of Chichén Itzá, and it experienced a final blossoming during the heyday of Mayapán.

A reconstruction of a so-called false-front house on Cozumel. From the front, all the walls appeared to be made of stone covered by heavy coats of plaster, when in fact only the front wall was so constructed. To save time and labor, the builders used wood for the side and back walls. Similar "false-front" houses were also found at Mayapán.

THE
EMERGENCE
OF
A
NEW
MODEL

*A painted scene from the Altar Vase found
in a Late Classic burial site at
Altar de Sacrificios.*

Our knowledge about the ancient Maya is growing rapidly from year to year. New projects abound, conferences and seminars on recent research flourish, publications pack the shelves of libraries, and graduate students flock to the subject. One has only to compare the first edition of Sylvanus Morley's *The Ancient Maya* published in 1946 with Robert Sharer's 1984 revision to see how radical the changes have been over the past four decades. Given shape by fresh discoveries, the new model of ancient Maya civilization that began to emerge in print by the late 1960s has fully crystallized in the past decade and a half.

The new model envisions a much more complex and dynamic Maya civilization. The elaborate social and economic systems were both considerably more complicated than earlier archaeologists had thought. In trade especially, the conventional view underestimated the heavy traffic in non-elite items and the range of Pre- and Postclassic exchange networks. The old and new models are in closer agreement regarding Classic Maya political conditions: local centers were the focus of power.

Archaeologists now realize that the Maya elite were not the uniform priestly rulers previously imagined. Joyce Marcus has insightfully noted that "hierarchies . . . can be based on political and administrative status, economic status, or ritual and religious status.

Carved elite figures ring this altar from Copán. Such elite personages had complex economic, political, and ideological roles in ancient Maya society.

Occasionally all three of these converge . . . but such cases are in the minority." She points out that the Maya political, religious, and economic hierarchies may not have been identical. A politically independent city ruled by its elite may have been part of a regional trading network controlled by outsiders.

I will now present a summary of the new model. Clearly, it is my own version. Although various Maya archaeologists almost certainly would disagree with different parts of it, I believe that it is a reasonable reading of the data currently available. Moreover, the continual onslaught of new publications on Maya archaeology make it a good bet that parts of this model will be out-of-date very shortly, if they are not already. My reading on this subject alone always seems to pile up no matter how diligent I am! But, far from discouraging me, the never-ending stream of new revelations is one of the reasons Maya studies is so exciting.

THE NEW SYNTHESIS

The Maya settlement of the lowlands began at the dawn of the first millennium B.C., if not earlier, when small agricultural villages were established by peoples from different parts of the adjacent highlands of what are now Guatemala and Chiapas, Mexico. Although scattered groups of hunters and gatherers had inhabited the lowlands for millennia, the first substantial settlement of the area apparently did not take place before 1200 or 1000 B.C. As the small villages gradually grew in population, groups split off to form new villages, filling in many of the empty zones in the lowland landscape over the next five hundred years. From the time of the first agricultural settlements, villages maintained widespread contacts through the trade of exotic materials like obsidian. There is even speculation that the Maya held regional fairs, which may have served as a means of communication as well.

As overall population mushroomed, more and more Mayans chose to live in the town centers instead of in the countryside. With the demographic growth came two significant trends: conflicts among centers increased as they began to compete for land, resources, and people, and large workforces were mobilized to undertake ambitious building projects. Throughout the preindustrial world, huge public construction often takes place early in complex cultural development, apparently, because it provides a means of solidifying and legitimating

This Late Preclassic urn was discovered in a rich burial beneath the North Acropolis at Tikal.

the power of burgeoning upper classes and, some have argued, of controlling the new large pools of urban population. The Tigre and Danta complexes at El Mirador, for example, appear to have been nearly as tall and large as any later building in the Southern Lowlands.

These two trends were critical factors in the development by about 300 B.C. of the first large towns and urban centers in the lowlands. Centers such as El Mirador, Tikal, Cuello, Lamanai, and Cerros in the Southern Lowlands and Dzibilchaltún and Komchén in the Northern Lowlands all grew substantially in population and area at this time. The Maya almost certainly introduced some forms of intensive agriculture to feed the larger populations. And they were inspired by the monumental art and hieroglyphic writing of the nearby highlands. The rise of Maya civilization can be traced to this time.

It was traditionally held that most of the cultural features that have been used to define the Classic period (A.D. 300–800)—particularly monumental architecture, hieroglyphic inscriptions, polychrome pottery, and large ceremonial centers—first appeared in the third century A.D. But, as we have seen, recent research has proved that many of the elements of complex society were present well before A.D. 300.

In the centuries that followed population continued to grow, spurring the establishment of new centers and the expansion of others. Population probably reached at least a million in the Southern Lowlands, and some scholars estimate that it might have been significantly higher. However, growth was neither continuous nor even all over the lowlands, as different sites had their ups and downs. Population growth and cultural development culminated during the Classic period and especially the Late Classic (A.D. 600–800).

The great cities at this time must have been impressive sights indeed, with huge acropoli of temples, palaces, ball courts, and courtyards. Large paved plazas gleamed white, while the plastered walls of the buildings ranged in hue from white to a gamut of colors including red and blue. Intricately carved stone monuments glorified the achievements of the rulers in pictures and words. The arts flourished in a variety of media, while the mathematical, astronomical, and linguistic attainments of the Maya reached new heights.

Many elite goods, such as the beautiful Late Classic polychrome vases, were produced in only a few cities, and these goods were exchanged all over the lowlands. In contrast, most utilitarian items, such as unslipped or monochrome storage jars, could be manufactured al-

most anywhere. These simpler items were traded within centers or among a regional group of centers. There is no strong archaeological evidence for markets, yet clearly both raw materials and finished products were moved over considerable distances. The exact mechanisms for such exchanges remain uncertain and may have varied for different goods. Various scholars have argued that the weight of evidence points to a lack of central economic control in Classic Maya civilization, meaning that the peasants were able to grow and manufacture what they pleased to sell how they pleased.

The complex Maya class structure apparently allowed great variation in wealth and access to material goods. The wealthy lived in the cities, especially toward the end of the Classic period, when only the poorer peasants were left in the countryside. Some cities became ever more crowded as a growing proportion of the population left full-time farming to become specialized workers in the urban centers, where they could labor on public works or pursue commercial ventures.

Left: Late Classic Maya artists created beautiful ornamental objects. Found in the Sacred *Cenote* at Chichén Itzá, this jade plaque from the late eighth century A.D. depicts a seated elite figure. Tatiana Proskouriakoff suggests that the plaque was thrown into the *Cenote* during a ceremony long after its creation. *Right:* This jade pendant dating to the sixth century A.D. has been interpreted as a dancing figure. The project organized by archaeologist David Pendergast discovered the pendant at the Southern Lowland site of Altun Ha, Belize.

The upper class gradually became more wealthy and powerful. The accelerated construction of "palaces" may mean that this group was taking on greater bureaucratic functions, including the organization of the larger labor forces and the management of food procurement and distribution for the increasing numbers of urban laborers. Decreasing public access to sacred areas may signal a widening gulf between the elite and the rest of society. As the Classic period progressed, the elite became more and more distanced from the middle and lower classes, speaking to commoners only in their roles as administrators or bureaucrats.

The Maya employed a wide variety of agricultural techniques to produce a number of crops. At first, animal meat was probably a significant part of the Maya diet, but by Classic times it was not eaten much, since animal habitats had been destroyed by expanding cities and the clearing of new lands for agriculture. Those living near rivers or the coast could eat fish or shellfish. Otherwise, the Maya diet was largely vegetarian.

The principal crop, maize, was supplemented by a number of other crops including beans and squashes. The Maya practiced extensive techniques of cultivation such as the slash-and-burn method, as well as a host of intensive techniques such as irrigation, the terracing and ridging of fields, and the reclamation of swampland. Gardens around houses, even close to the urban cores, also provided needed foodstuffs. Orchards for the breadnut and various fruits may have helped feed the Maya as well.

Religion permeated every aspect of ancient Maya life. From a modern perspective, nothing was "secular" in Maya life, at least in the realm of the elite, and there was no separation of church and state. The demands of the gods were harsh, and Maya rituals included human sacrifices. The rulers subjected themselves to considerable self-mutilation—for example, by rasping blood from their bodies with spiny vines or sharp sting-ray spines. The popular ball game was not only a competitive sport but a sacred ceremony in which basic myths were reenacted, particularly the battle between the mythic "hero twins" and the lords of the underworld. It was played by individuals or two small teams in a special court with parallel sloping or vertical sides. The heavily padded players attempted to strike a hard rubber ball with their bodies through a stone ring mounted on the side of the playing wall. In some versions, they hit a carved stone marker. The use of hands or feet to hit the ball was strictly forbidden. On special

This drawing by archaeologist Ian Graham of Lintel 24 at Yaxchilán shows a ruler rasping her tongue for blood during a religious ritual.

occasions, the losing captain or team might be sacrificed at the conclusion of the game.

From before the time of Christ, rulers and their cities vied for control of land, resources, and people by means of raiding and warfare. By the Late Classic, such conflict may have been rampant. The Maya may have forced captured prisoners to join the labor forces that constructed the raised fields, monumental buildings, and roads, or the captives may have been put to death during sacrificial ceremonies.

Although clothed in ritual, such conflicts also had their critical material side. Political fortunes seem to have waxed and waned, and little strong evidence exists that any one city built long-standing control over a large region. In fact, the ambiguous data may indicate either that individual centers had political control over large parts of the lowlands or that cities held sway over only small territories in their immediate environs. Although elegant and stimulating models have been built, especially ones based on hieroglyphic inscriptions, to argue for very different political scenarios, Maya government remains unclear.

The Great Ball Court at Chichén Itzá had vertical sides holding high stone rings.

Bound, captive figures carved on monuments, such as this Late Classic altar from Tikal, are just one indication of widespread raiding in the lowlands.

What is clear is that by the beginning of the eighth century A.D., a number of factors were creating mounting strains on both Maya society and its environment in the Southern Lowlands. To provide food for the rising population, the Maya escalated the clearing of forests. The demand for nonagricultural labor grew, luring farmers away from the land. Conflicts between centers became more frequent, and outsiders began threatening the western frontier of the lowlands.

Between A.D. 750 and 850, many cities in the Southern Lowlands stopped constructing large buildings and carving monumental sculpture. The population at some cities declined drastically, while others were completely abandoned. This collapse was an extremely complicated process, and it is now clear that it was limited in scope. Maya civilization as a whole did not collapse, and the abandonment was limited to a large part, but not all, of the Southern Lowlands. Nevertheless, where it occurred the collapse was dramatic and relatively sudden. It was also permanent, as there was little or no subsequent recovery.

Although the precise trigger for the fall of the great southern cities remains elusive, its general causes can be outlined. The foundation of Classic Maya civilization was its agricultural system. As the population grew and the ratio of nonagricultural workers to full-time food producers increased, that system must have come under enormous pressure. Attempts to further intensify agriculture may well have ruined the soil. Fragmentary evidence indicates that malnutrition may have become a problem at this time. Furthermore, the Maya may have been at a loss to manage the problems created by the mushrooming urban, agricultural, and military demands, and the apparent decrease in social mobility meant that the most able people could not be recruited into the ranks of the elite leadership. The many pressures could have made Maya society vulnerable to any social or ecological perturbation. If a severe drought occurred at this time, as some archaeologists have recently argued, then it could have been the final straw.

Yet, at the same time that the Maya were abandoning many Southern Lowland cities, centers in the Northern Lowlands of the Yucatán Peninsula were beginning a great florescence. The huge city of Chichén Itzá and the well-known Puuc cities of Uxmal, Kabah, and Sayil initiated massive construction programs as their populations soared. Sites along the east coast and in northern Belize began to flourish, or at least showed no sign of decline. Many residents also remained at centers in the lake district of the Southern Lowlands south of Tikal, and at a few cities along the western and southeastern borders of the Southern Lowlands, several of which may have prospered under the occupation of invaders from the Gulf Coast lowlands.

Thus, while it appears that most large centers in the Southern Lowlands had ceased to function by the end of the ninth century, centers in other parts of the lowlands were still alive and thriving. There was no massive, overall collapse but a partial one, leading to large-scale demographic, political, and economic rearrangements. The Classic tradition did not die out entirely, but its focus shifted from the Southern to the Northern Lowlands.

Whatever the immediate causes of the collapse, the reason the Southern Lowlands never recovered appears to have been economic. The Classic Maya were skilled artisans who produced goods that were traded over a vast area, but they did not control many important resources. Many centers that did survive the ninth century were in regions such as northern Belize that had good soil and climate for

Elaborate cut stone mosaics found on the upper facades of buildings are among the features of Puuc architecture. This mosaic on the Great Palace at Sayil represents the god of rain.

growing the highly prized cacao bean, or they were in the coastal areas of the Northern Lowlands, which could produce salt. The particularly fertile soils of the Puuc region could support dense populations without the same degree of agricultural intensification that was necessary in most places in the south.

Along with Chichén Itzá, the Puuc region cities reached their heyday during the Terminal Classic period from about A.D. 800 to 1000, although Chichén Itzá probably remained important for another century or two. In general, the architecture, arts, city planning, and material goods of these centers were similar to those of the Classic cities in the Southern Lowlands. Exchanges with Central Mexico remained as lively as ever, although it is not certain whether the contacts were direct or through intermediaries such as the Chontal Maya of the Gulf Coast lowlands. Obsidian from Central Mexico was traded to Yucatán, while Maya and Central Mexican art and architecture each influenced the other. There is no strong evidence, however, that the Toltecs of Central Mexico conquered Chichén Itzá or even visited Yucatán.

Eventually the Puuc region sites fell into oblivion, for reasons that are not clear. Quite possibly the Puuc centers lost out to Chichén Itzá

The Castillo, a huge temple-pyramid at Chichén Itzá.

in a prolonged struggle for economic control of Yucatán. In any case, Chichén Itzá ultimately suffered a severe political and economic decline, too. By A.D. 1200, if not earlier, construction ceased and the city center fell into disuse. Without large-scale settlement data, it is impossible to know what happened to Chichén Itzá's population at this time. Even though the center was not completely abandoned and in fact served as a major shrine for religious pilgrimages until the time of the Spanish Conquest, its downfall brought the Classic tradition to a close.

With the fall of Chichén Itzá, the city of Mayapán rose to prominence. In effect, Mayapán replaced Chichén Itzá as the political and economic center of Yucatán from A.D. 1250 to 1450. In some cases, its inhabitants even attempted to replicate the architecture of Chichén Itzá, although on a smaller scale. Yet despite a few similarities, Mayapán is vastly different from its predecessor. It can be argued that Mayapán's rise marks the dividing line between the Classic and Postclassic periods.

As the capital of a confederacy that spanned much of the Northern Lowlands, Mayapán controlled a series of provinces, each with its own local government. Members of the leading families of these provinces were required to live at Mayapán, thus assuring the ruling elite at the capital of the loyalty of the subject provinces.

Mayapán was quite different in appearance from earlier Maya centers. It was much more compact—its approximately 12,000 inhabitants lived in a 4-square-kilometer area surrounded by a stone wall. The wall protected the city from attack during the many conflicts between the cities of the confederacy that characterized the period. While the art and architecture of the time clearly were less impressive than those of the Classic period, both the political and economic systems appear to have been complex and vigorous. On the east coast of

A view from the sea of the Late Postclassic site of Tulum.

the Yucatán Peninsula, archaeologists have found that politically independent centers such as San Gervasio on the Island of Cozumel,
Tulum, Tancah, and Xelhá, as well as Lamanai and Santa Rita in
Belize, flourished during this late period and that most had ties with
Mayapán. They also actively participated in extensive long-distance
trade, not only with Mayapán, but with centers as far away as Naco in
Honduras and Xicalango on the Gulf Coast. For some goods, as with
cotton and cacao from Belize or honey and salt from the coast, they
acted as producers, while for others, as with hard stone from the highlands, they were the middlemen.

A map showing the far-flung trade networks
of the Late Postclassic period.

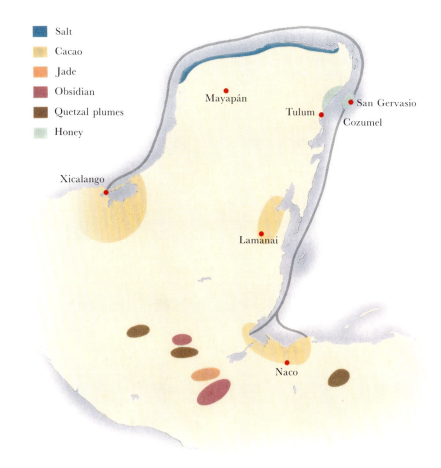

Salt

Cacao

Jade

Obsidian

Quetzal plumes

Honey

Mayapán

Tulum

San Gervasio

Cozumel

Xicalango

Lamanai

Naco

According to art historian Flora Clancy, this Late Postclassic incense burner from Mayapán represents the feathered serpent Quetzalcoatl in human guise. Its parts may have been mass-produced.

After the decline of Mayapán in the mid-fifteenth century, due in part to political intrigues and internecine warfare, no single dominant city emerged to take its place as it had replaced Chichén Itzá. Yucatán rapidly became divided into a series of independent provinces. It was this decentralized society that the early Spanish explorers encountered in the second decade of the sixteenth century.

CURRENT RESEARCH

The swift pace of archaeological research in the Maya lowlands is one sign of the exciting nature of Maya archaeology today. A host of contemporary field projects and laboratory analyses, as well as studies on the frontiers of hieroglyphic and historic research, will already have challenged a few aspects of my model by the time this book is published. Examples of projects now underway are the research of Richard E. W. Adams and his team at Rio Azul and the continuing work of Juan Pedro Laporte and other Guatemalan archaeologists at Tikal, as well as the research just commencing at Dos Pilas under the directorship of Arthur Demarest and Stephen Houston; research in Belize including the work of Diane and Arlen Chase at Caracol, Tom Hester, Harry Shafer, and their colleagues at Colha, the regional research of Richard Leventhal, Anabel Ford's intersite Belize River survey, and Joe Ball and his team in the Mopan-Macal triangle; and research in the Northern Lowlands like that of Bill Ringle and his associates at Ek Balam. Other projects have just been completed, such as the long-term, intensive fieldwork of David Pendergast and the Royal Ontario Museum at Lamanai, and their write-ups promise to have a huge impact on the current model. All these projects, and more, deserve extended discussion in any treatment of modern directions in Maya research. But to illustrate the directions research is taking today, I will focus on three projects: the large multiteam research effort at Copán, the investigations at Isla Cerritos, and the Sayil Archaeological Project.

THE SAYIL ARCHAEOLOGICAL PROJECT

I launched the Sayil Archaeological Project in 1983 to undertake the first full-scale settlement study of one of the great centers of the Puuc region. Gair Tourtellot joined me the following year as codirector of the project, which has completed five field seasons of fieldwork (from 1983 to 1988) with the support of the National Science Foundation.

In my initial proposal to the N.S.F. in 1982, I pointed out that the Terminal Classic period was a time of crisis and transformation for ancient Maya civilization. The Classic Maya centers in the south collapsed, the sites in the hilly Puuc region of the Northern Lowlands were prospering, and Chichén Itzá began its rise to prominence. While recently much attention has been paid to the collapse in the south, a large corpus of published materials on the rise of the north has been lacking. We needed to see the other side of the coin. If we could study the growth of centers in the Puuc region, we might be able to learn more about what happened during the collapse.

I went on to query: What were the populations of the major Puuc region sites? Were the sites urban centers? How did the populations change from Late Classic to Postclassic times? Given the changing economic patterns of the Terminal Classic period, would the settlements of the Puuc zone differ from earlier Classic settlements? Is it at all possible to find any material evidence in the Puuc region for political control of the coastal salt trade? Is an influx of peoples from the Southern Lowlands into the north visible in the settlement record? Are "foreign" influences, such as Chontal Maya, Toltec, or Oaxacan, present in the Puuc region settlements? What was the relationship between peoples in the Puuc region and those at Chichén Itzá? It was clear that none of these questions could be answered without intensive settlement pattern studies at Puuc region sites, nor could general hypotheses about the growth of Maya civilization be proposed and tested. Unfortunately, although much was known about the great architecture in the core areas of famous Puuc sites such as Uxmal, Kabah, Sayil, and Labná, which draw a multitude of tourists every year, surprisingly little was known about the size, extent, or nature of the settlements around these centers.

My interest in the settlement of the Puuc region was a direct outgrowth of my work on two earlier projects. At Seibal I had examined the collapse of Classic Maya civilization in the Southern Lowlands and at the Island of Cozumel I had researched the changing nature of ancient Maya trade and its relation to the development of Maya civilization. Both the Seibal and Cozumel research were also concerned with the spread of the mercantile-oriented Chontal Maya from the Gulf Coast lowlands into the lowland Maya realm. The Puuc region would be an ideal choice for studies that could follow up many of the questions raised by these earlier researches.

After visiting a number of Puuc sites in 1982 and conferring with officials in the Mexican National Institute of Anthropology and History, I decided, with the Institute's approval, that Sayil, which is situated in the core of the eastern Puuc region, about halfway between Kabah and Labná, would present the best opportunity for long-term research in the region. The site was relatively undisturbed: Sayil had not had the tourist development that Uxmal and Kabah had, and relatively little modern settlement or agriculture had tampered with the area around it. During the dry season, there is reasonably unobscured vision in the uncleared areas surrounding Sayil, and the bushes and trees do not obscure the archaeological features, as does the vegetation around the western Puuc sites such as Oxkintok, where there has been a lot of recent agricultural activity. Another bonus was the existence of a good map of Sayil's major standing architecture, made in 1934 by Edwin Shook, which could serve as a base map of the settlement study. Finally, according to previous studies the bulk of the occupation and visible architecture at Sayil probably dated to the relatively short time span of the Terminal Classic period. I had considered working at Oxkintok, for example, but it had a significant Classic period occupation that would have made it much more difficult to analyze the visible settlement.

I have already described our mapping procedures. The Sayil maps are of particular interest because of the amount of detail. Because the platforms of ancient perishable dwellings were unusually well preserved, we were able to map the floor plans in exceptional detail. Settlement is indicated not by black squares or rectangles but by outlines of platforms that precisely depict room alignments and attached stone walls. The maps indicate local topography in 1-meter contour intervals and chart major soil changes.

My colleagues and I are now analyzing the findings of five field seasons from 1983 to 1988. The preliminary results support our working hypothesis that Sayil was occupied for a relatively short time, almost exclusively during the Terminal Classic period. We have found clear indications that Sayil was a city, definite settlement boundaries for the urban zone, and evidence for settlement in the areas between major Puuc centers. Approximately 10,000 people or slightly fewer lived in the urban core, and another 7,000 people lived in the suburbs. When we compared our estimates of the population with the produc-

tivity of the soils, we discovered that by about A.D. 900 the population of Sayil had nearly reached the carrying capacity of its land. This finding may be an important clue as we investigate the reasons for Sayil's rapid demise.

In the 1987 and 1988 field seasons we undertook intensive surface collections on, around, and between a number of domestic platforms. We divided the collection areas into 2-by-2-meter squares and carefully picked up by hand all the materials on the surface of each square. Our findings should allow project members to better understand the internal socioeconomic make-up of Sayil and to examine a number of issues relating to elite and peasant lifeways, including questions

The three-story Great Palace is the best-known structure at Sayil.

Careful control of surface collections was an essential part of the research strategy of the Sayil Archaeological Project.

about how the domestic units grew through time and what some of the material and behavioral differences between the elite and peasantry were like. These detailed collections, along with soil phosphate analyses, have allowed us to identify what were probably garden plots around house platforms. Perhaps Sayil (and other Maya cities?) was a "garden city." This finding has important implications for the economic organization of Sayil and the relative economic independence of the population. If many city dwellers had direct access to at least some foodstuffs, then at least some limits would have been placed on the coercive power of Sayil's rulers.

To date there is little evidence in ceramics, architecture, or settlement that the Chontal Maya actually visited or settled Sayil, nor is there evidence that peoples from the Southern Lowlands migrated to Sayil at the start of its florescence around A.D. 800. However, some architectural and ceramic styles hint that the first settlers of Sayil may have come from the region just to the south, which in turn might have been under indirect demographic pressure from further south as many major Southern Lowlands centers collapsed.

Last, but certainly not least, we examined the underground cis-terns (*chultunes*) at Sayil. These cisterns provided the drinking water that permitted the Maya to survive in the agriculturally rich but water-poor Puuc region. We are hoping to learn what groups had cis-terns, and thus direct access to water, and what groups did not. We would also like to know how and if the groups with cisterns changed through time. Patricia McAnany has estimated the population of Sayil's urban core based on the number and size of the cisterns. Her figures are very similar to the ones generated by domestic room counts.

The Sayil Archaeological Project is an example of a project cen-tered on one site that combines both surface survey and excavation and that attempts to look at the site in the context of its wider sustain-ing area. It focused on peasant remains in the hope that settlement patterns would reveal the organization and function of the community of Sayil. The first two phases of the project, mapping/surface survey and excavation, spanned five years—long enough to map the site in detail and to investigate a sample of its zones, yet short enough not to

The narrow mouth of a *chultun* at Sayil. The Maya built cisterns for year-round survival in the Puuc region where permanent water sources were scarce.

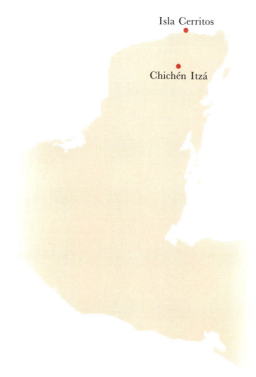

Isla Cerritos

Chichén Itzá

produce so much material that we could never examine it all in a reasonable number of years. Moreover, the number of archaeologists, graduate students, and workers was never so large that the directors had to spend more time doing administration than archaeology. Tourtellot and I were fortunate in having a first-hand understanding of all the active fieldwork and laboratory work we directed.

THE ISLA CERRITOS ARCHAEOLOGICAL PROJECT

The Isla Cerritos Archaeological Project was initiated by Anthony Andrews, Tomás Gallareta Negron, Fernando Robles Castellanos, and Rafael Cobos Palma in 1984. These archaeologists planned to test the hypothesis that the island was the main coastal port of Chichén Itzá. The preliminary results of their 1984 and 1985 research, as well as follow-up surveys, have given firm support to this hypothesis.

An aerial view of Isla Cerritos off the northern coast of Yucatán. Note the remains of the seawall, which are visible to the left of the island.

The project's intensive survey of the island soon confirmed it had indeed been a port. The archaeologists found a seawall complete with two entryways (one of which was flanked by platforms), and they discovered the remains of what apparently were docks and jetties or piers. Excavations revealed that much of the island had been artificially built up over time to provide more room for a variety of structures.

The ceramic and other artifacts uncovered by the project also supported the trading port hypothesis. The majority of the obsidian found at Isla Cerritos came from Central Mexico, while a smaller percentage originated in the Maya highlands and elsewhere. Other exotic materials found on the island included a gold artifact from Central America, greenstone from the Maya highlands, and turquoise from Northern Mexico.

So, if Isla Cerritos appeared to have been a port, was it Chichén Itzá's port? Judging by ceramic studies, ties to Chichén Itzá seem to have been close; archaeologists have found that many ceramics at Isla

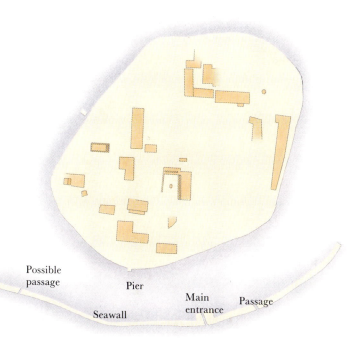

Possible passage

Pier

Seawall

Main entrance

Passage

A map of the structures found on Isla Cerritos, drawn by the Isla Cerritos Archaeological Project.

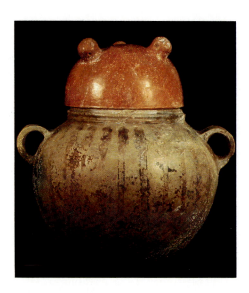

Archaeologists found this typical Chichén Red tripod bowl directly on top of this Muna Slate jar during their excavations on Isla Cerritos. The bowl is characteristic of Chichén Itzá pottery, while the jar is typical of Puuc styles.

Cerritos are similar to those from Chichén Itzá. The heyday of Isla Cerritos coincided almost exactly with the florescence of Chichén Itzá, and the two centers appear to have declined at the same time in the early thirteenth century A.D.

The Isla Cerritos Archaeological Project is a nice example of a class of small, highly productive, problem-oriented projects that are beginning to grow in number and importance in Maya studies. Scholars identify particular problems in Maya archaeology, then construct research strategies to resolve them. These projects are relatively easy to carry out: only a few seasons in the field are usually needed, costs are modest, and the subsequent analyses and publication can be performed relatively quickly.

RESEARCH AT COPÁN

The recent archaeological research at the famous Southern Lowland site of Copán in Honduras is a very good example of a kind of study that has become popular elsewhere in Mesoamerica. A large site and its surrounding region are tackled not by one institution and director but by a series of scholars and institutions. Different aspects of the research are "subcontracted" to different archaeologists or divided up among a group of them. The continuing research at Copán was initiated in 1975 by the government of Honduras—first under the direction of Gordon Willey and subsequently under Claude Baudez and then William Sanders. Its twin goals are to enhance the tourist trade by restoring temples and palaces and to understand the city's ancient growth and development.

Archaeologists at Copán have focused on restoring the elite structures at the core of the site, deciphering the hieroglyphic inscriptions in the core, and examining the settlement, both suburban and rural, throughout the Copán Valley. The impressive array of Maya scholars who have participated in the project include Baudez, William Fash, Richard Leventhal, Sanders, Linda Schele, Robert Sharer, David Stuart, David Webster, and Willey, among many others. I would like to illustrate here just two small examples of the extensive work at Copán: one piece of research on the elite and one focusing on the remains of the peasants.

William Fash of Northern Illinois University and his associates have been studying the Hieroglyphic Stairway and Temple (known

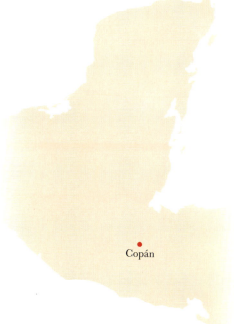

Copán

The Hieroglyphic Stairway at Copán.

more prosaically as Structure 10L-26). Their work is an excellent illustration of how hieroglyphic research and dirt archaeology can work hand in hand to produce richer insights into ancient Maya cultural development than either approach could produce by itself. The Hieroglyphic Stairway and Temple consists of a temple surmounting a pyramid, whose front stairway has hieroglyphic inscriptions carved on its risers. The structure had been excavated by the Peabody Museum in the 1890s and partially restored in the 1930s by the Carnegie Institution of Washington. Over the years, many of the stones with hieroglyphic inscriptions had fallen from their original positions. By inspecting old photographs as well as by matching up neighboring stones jigsaw-puzzle fashion, Fash and his coworkers were able to piece together the original inscriptions. As Fash discusses in a 1988 article, "A New Look at Maya Statecraft from Copán, Honduras," these inscriptions were particularly fascinating because they dated from a critical time in Copán's history.

New readings of Copán inscriptions, as well as those of the nearby site of Quiriguá, had indicated that in A.D. 737 the important Copán ruler known as XVIII Jog, who had led the city for more than half a century, was captured in battle by the ruler of Quiriguá and decapitated. Immediately after the demise of XVIII Jog, the Maya constructed the Hieroglyphic Stairway of Structure 10L-26 and rebuilt the temple atop the structure for the seventh time. Fash was particularly interested in seeing if Quiriguá took control of Copán after its great victory or if Copán made a comeback and reasserted the primacy of its

A closer view of the Hieroglyphic Stairway shows carved inscriptions on the risers.

royal lineage. The newly reconstructed stairway inscription told of a new ruler's inauguration at Copán soon after XVIII Jog's death. This ruler belonged to Copán's traditional royal line, and so the inscriptions reaffirmed the legitimacy of Copán's royalty. There were no indications that Quiriguá lorded it over Copán.

This reading of the hieroglyphs was reinforced by two lines of archaeological evidence, one from the research at Structure 10L-26, the other from general excavation and survey data from both Copán and Quiriguá. Artifacts from the two sites were stylistically distinct in the period after A.D. 737, indicating that the two cities probably remained autonomous after XVIII Jog's decapitation. In response to their defeat, the Copán elite made conscious attempts to glorify the new leadership of Copán and its warriors. A cache under the altar in front of the Hieroglyphic Stairway was found to contain two jade plaque heirlooms that glorified earlier members of the Copán dynasty. On rebuilding the crowning temple after XVIII Jog's death, Copán artists decorated the previously plain outer walls with imposing figures of Copán warriors as if to say "we are still the greatest." Thus, both hieroglyphic and archaeological data seem to agree that the rulers of Copán made a huge attempt to reassert their earlier greatness after their shattering defeat by a smaller neighbor.

Not all the work at Copán has centered on the site core and the elite. In the 1970s, Gordon Willey and Richard Leventhal undertook a settlement survey and intensive excavations in the zone around Copán, while more recently William Sanders, David Webster, and their colleagues have been studying the rural zones in the Copán Valley well away from the great site. In a fascinating 1988 article entitled "Household Remains of the Humblest Maya," David Webster and Nancy Gonlin discuss the preliminary results of their excavations of eight separate rural domestic remains.

Webster and Gonlin's research is especially noteworthy because their efforts were directed at remains that were both rural in location and small in size. They excavated domestic platforms located from 2.2 to 22 kilometers away from the core of the city, and no platform they excavated was more than 1.2 meters in height. Webster and Gonlin did not excavate by placing small test pits in the center of the remains, as has often done in the past; instead, they exposed large horizontal surfaces by stripping away all the surface overburdens. They were able to obtain precise dates for the artifacts through obsidian hydration dating, a technique that can date obsidian objects to within decades in

Excavations of domestic structures in the rural zones of the Copán Valley by David Webster and his team have helped clarify archaeologists' understandings of the development of Copán.

contrast to the much grosser ceramic dating that gives only the century of manufacture at best.

Obsidian hydration dating is becoming more popular in Maya studies. In this procedure, researchers measure in microscopic detail the build-up of a "rind" on obsidian artifacts over the centuries. If the average modern temperature and moisture are known in the zone where the obsidian was found and if these measurements can be reliably projected back in time, the thickness of the rind will tell the age of the artifact. Since scholars have succeeded in refining the measurement scales, they have been obtaining dates with apparently small margins of error in some regions of the Maya lowlands. When archaeologists can recover a high number of obsidian artifacts, then it is possible—as it has been at Copán—to construct a very exact chronology.

By dating the rural structures, Webster and Gonlin were able to learn that the more distant rural areas were not colonized to any significant degree until the eighth century A.D., when population build-up at Copán pushed farmers out into the further reaches of the Copán Valley. The dating, along with the results of pollen analyses, also suggests that the rural zones were not abandoned a century later, around A.D. 800, when the central core collapsed. This finding could mean that when the Maya abandoned city centers, they did not necessarily abandon the entire city. Some centers, because of the resources they controlled or because of their strategic location along trade routes or for other reasons, may have maintained sizable populations even though their civic-religious cores were deserted.

ARCHAEOLOGY
AND
THE
MODERN
WORLD

The Dove Cotes building at the Puuc site
of Uxmal.

*I*n some sense, archaeologists dwell in two worlds, the past and the present. Their aim is to understand a culture from the past, but their vision of that culture is touched in many ways by the vogues and lifestyles of the present. Archaeologists cannot escape the biases of modern society, but they can try to control the influence of those biases by acknowledging them. Yet the influences of the present are not necessarily invalid. Archaeologists recognize that human civilizations share much in common. Our views of the present may sometimes give insight into the past, and conversely, civilizations of the past may shed light on the present.

CHANGING PERSPECTIVES IN ARCHAEOLOGY

In recent years, some scholars have been casting a critical eye at how Western culture has influenced the thinking of archaeologists. Clearly, archaeologists are not unbiased observers of the past, collecting completely objective data about the archaeological record. It was not too long ago, for example, that Maya archaeologists did not "see" peasant house mounds because they were not perceived as "important." And we can be certain that archaeologists in the not-too-distant future will shake their heads in disbelief at some of the assumptions and procedures of contemporary scholars.

One of the most perceptive observers of modern-day caprices is the archaeologist Richard Wilk. In a 1985 article entitled "The Ancient Maya and the Political Present," Wilk examines the recent writings of a host of U.S. Mayanists, especially those that have appeared in a series of influential edited volumes on the development of Maya civilization. He found that new explanations of the Classic Maya "collapse" mirrored important political concerns in the United States. Archaeologists were blaming warfare and conquest for the collapse just as the Vietnam conflict was escalating in the late 1960s. Then, when the environmental movement began raising the alarm in the early 1970s, archaeologists revived an earlier argument suggesting that the Maya had misused the lowland soil. During the religious revival of the 1970s suddenly Maya ideology became important in collapse hypotheses—including suggestions that ancient Maya religious prophecies foretelling their own doom had created a fatalism in the Maya that weakened their will to survive. While Wilk's correlations are interesting, they do not prove that current intellectual trends de-

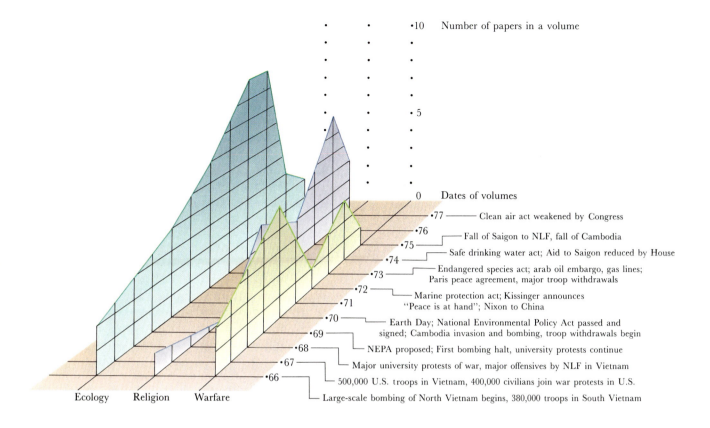

Number of papers in a volume

•10

•5

0   Dates of volumes

•77 ——— Clean air act weakened by Congress

•76 ————— Fall of Saigon to NLF, fall of Cambodia

•75 ————— Safe drinking water act; Aid to Saigon reduced by House

•74 ————— Endangered species act; arab oil embargo, gas lines;
              Paris peace agreement, major troop withdrawals

•73

•72 ——— Marine protection act; Kissinger announces
              "Peace is at hand"; Nixon to China

•71

•70 ——— Earth Day; National Environmental Policy Act passed and
              signed; Cambodia invasion and bombing, troop withdrawals begin

•69

•68 ——— NEPA proposed; First bombing halt, university protests continue

•67 ——— Major university protests of war, major offensives by NLF in Vietnam

•66 ——— 500,000 U.S. troops in Vietnam, 400,000 civilians join war protests in U.S.

—— Large-scale bombing of North Vietnam begins, 380,000 troops in South Vietnam

Ecology   Religion   Warfare

termine which views of the collapse become popular, nor is there any-thing necessarily "wrong" about archaeologists letting political trends influence their thinking. However, if his correlations are valid, they indicate how careful scholars must be to ensure that current biases are not blinding them to alternative hypotheses or limiting the kinds of data they collect. As Wilk cogently suggests, "Archaeological dis-course has a dual nature: at the same time that it pursues objective, verifiable knowledge about the past, it also conducts an informal and often hidden political and philosophical debate about the major issues of contemporary life. . . . The task is to recognize the nature of the dialogue and to take responsibility for it."

Perhaps the most overarching change in focus in Maya studies has been a shift from an upper-class or elitist perspective to a broader point of view. Archaeologists now try to give equal importance to all levels of Maya society, from the peasant to the artisan to the ruler. It is essential to emphasize that even though not all traditional Mayanists were upper class, many were, and the overwhelming major-

Richard Wilk noted these correlations between recent political concerns in the United States and popular explanations of the Classic Maya collapse.

Scholars can now read most Maya hiero-glyphs such as those on this Piedras Negras stela depicting a ruler's accession, deciphered by Tatiana Proskouriakoff in the early 1960s. Its content is typical of the elite concerns that dominate Maya writings.

ity focused their studies on their elite Maya counterparts. On the other hand, the Maya researchers of the past two decades come from many different classes and backgrounds.

After World War II, but especially in the 1960s, a new wave of scholars entered the field of archaeology. Most of these individuals were neither wealthy nor from upper-class backgrounds. Thanks to funding from the National Science Foundation and other new sources, anyone had the chance to carry out his or her own field project on the Maya. Many more positions for archaeologists became available throughout the country, particularly at state universities. The entire face of Maya studies changed. Now students from modest and even poor origins could afford to enter archaeology, which had once been almost a hobby of the rich. These archaeologists brought to their re-search new interests from their varied backgrounds, perhaps farming or factory work, for example. Because of their broader outlook, archae-ologists were more willing to look at the ancient Maya not as some-thing unique but as similar to preindustrial civilizations all over the globe. And many new archaeologists brought to their field suspicions of elite values, or even outright hostility.

In contrast to their predecessors, many archaeologists today are fascinated by the ordinary objects left by peasants and by their manu-facture and distribution. They use methodologies that explore the common lifeways, such as the settlement pattern research that maps and excavates peasant houses along with elite ones. In assessing cul-ture change, they consider not only high art and architecture but tech-nology, agriculture, and trade. Modern scholars don't look at artifacts and buildings as isolated pieces; they consider entire sites and regions as objects of scrutiny. Now that archaeologists are able to value the contributions of peasants and workers, they are looking at the Pre- and Postclassic periods with new interest and respect. They appreciate that although Postclassic elite art and architecture certainly were not as accomplished as Classic, most Maya lived better, and the economic and political systems were quite complex.

It is not too much to say that the broader perspective of post–World War II archaeology led to the current, multifaceted view of the ancient Maya world. Archaeologists are hard at work testing different parts of the new model and adding or correcting details. But just as the new perspective is beginning to come into its own, it has come under attack by a new elite position, albeit one that is more sophisticated and more flexible than that of the past. The new elitism is inspired by important breakthroughs in the decipherment of Maya hieroglyphic writing. The hieroglyphic texts are now revealing much that was unknowable before about wars between centers and royal marriages between leading families. The danger is that archaeologists will draw new conclusions about the Maya that are based solely on these hieroglyphics, which could be the mendacious or fanciful boasting of Maya rulers. Maya warfare or political domination will never be clearly understood without examining all levels of ancient Maya life.

Although the new, more egalitarian perspective may prove barren or unproductive in the long run, it remains only partly tested yet promising. It would be sad to see it compromised before it has had an opportunity to show its potential.

LESSONS FROM THE MAYA COLLAPSE

Many people have the impression that when it comes to the modern world, archaeologists have their heads stuck in the sand like ostriches, so wrapped in what happened in the past that they are oblivious to what is going on in the present. But such is not the case. On the contrary, a number of scholars believe that their studies are relevant to problems facing people today. These archaeologists, myself included, suggest that we can learn from examining the fates of earlier civilizations.

I do not have the nerve to claim that archaeologists can successfully predict the future or that they should be advising policymakers in Washington. Nor do I believe that archaeological understandings of cultural development can in the normal course of events directly influence political decisions. However, by comparing our modern society with earlier civilizations, we may see more clearly the likely results of trends such as the destruction of tropical rainforests and the rapid shrinking of the farming population in the United States. The "lessons of history" cannot necessarily tell us exactly what tack to follow today, but they can teach us what courses of action have succeeded or failed in the past and why.

Maya studies offer good examples of how the mistakes of the past can shed light on the problems of today. I have long argued that some troubling parallels can be found between the modern world and Classic Maya civilization just before its decline. One such parallel is the destruction of the rainforests throughout the world today and in the

Modern Agriculture in tropical climates relies on many of the same techniques used by the ancient Maya. Here a forest is being burned to provide farmland.

southern Yucatán Peninsula of A.D. 800. Can this analogy teach us anything?

Archaeologists Don Rice of the University of Virginia and Prudence Rice of the University of Florida wrote a superb article in 1984, entitled "Lessons from the Maya," pointing out that by carefully studying the effects of deforestation in the Southern Lowlands throughout the Classic period, we can discover the long-term consequences of clearing vast tracts of rainforest. Unlike modern ecological research, which can only study change over decades, archaeological studies can look at results over hundreds of years. These studies suggest that as the Maya cleared away the rainforest, they deprived the thin soils of their protective cover. With no thick foliage to deflect the sun's rays, the soils soon lost their nutrients to the hot tropical sun. Yet because the rapidly growing population needed to be fed, I would argue that the Maya couldn't afford any longer to leave fields fallow and unproductive until they recovered. By using fields year after year, they may have increased erosion and depleted the soil of its minerals. Eventually either the land just gave out or production was so poor that an otherwise minor shock, such as a drought or a war during harvest,

left the Maya without reserves. Their choice may have been leave or starve.

On the positive side, the Rices point out that the Maya successfully exploited the tropical rainforest for over 1,500 years, and for many centuries during that period they farmed the rainforest land heavily. By analyzing Maya agricultural techniques and their impacts on the environment, we can perhaps better understand the reasons for both long-lasting success and ultimate failure. This knowledge could be the key to avoiding catastrophe.

A second parallel between ourselves and the Maya is a trend that also contributed to the failure of the Maya agricultural system. At a time when population was growing, many Maya were leaving full-time agricultural production to become urban workers, deserting rural homes to live in the city. Fewer and fewer farmers were being asked to support more and more people. To keep up with the enormous demand for food, the Maya had to increase the yield per farmer. One way they did so was by reclaiming the rich land of the swamps. This worked fine for a while, but eventually that land may have been depleted as well. The lush swamp vegetation that had continually re-

These eroded and deforested hills of modern Madagascar give just a glimpse of what may come to pass on a global scale through destruction of tropical forests.

Understanding the successes and failures of Classic Maya agriculture may provide a useful perspective on current farming trends in the United States, such as the loss of small farms and the rise of large agribusiness.

freshed the soil had been cleared away, leaving the hot sun to do its work. The final result was no better than the clearing of the rainforest.

The clearing of the rainforest and the reclamation of swampland both ultimately failed, and for the same reason. The lowlands of the Yucatán Peninsula could not support the numbers of Maya living there. Does the same fate await nations that are even now destroying their rainforest to feed their multiplying hungry? And if so, will other countries of the world, perhaps our own, one day follow them?

Americans in particular have great faith in the ability of technological innovation to save us in times of crisis. We don't have to worry about overpopulation or dying farms because when push comes to shove, something like hydroponics will emerge to provide enough food. Yet in the case of the Classic Maya, few significant technological innovations occurred during the critical period before the collapse. With metal-cutting tools, for example, farmers could have cleared fields more rapidly and produced more crops, at least in the short term. But although metallurgy was just being introduced from Central America at the time, metal objects appeared only in religious ceremonies. Is our faith in technological rescue misplaced and dangerous, and can we afford to rely so heavily on its promise?

Although we have unlimited confidence in our own ingenuity and foresight, it can be difficult to guard against a rigidity of thinking that may blind us to fresh solutions. Once again, the case of the Maya is instructive. There are many indications that the Maya elite were aware of the threats to their way of life in the century before the collapse. For example, they intensified their efforts to reclaim more swampland. Yet, with the luxury of hindsight, we can see that one of their principal responses to the crisis seems to have exacerbated the problems. Within the world view of the time, it assuredly made sense to build newer and larger monuments to glorify the gods, who might then intercede on behalf of the beleagured cities. Perhaps the Maya also felt that by demonstrating wealth and strength to hostile neighbors, the impressive buildings would gain the city an edge in regional conflicts. However, the ambitious building projects actually accelerated the decline, by drawing more resources and people from agriculture and by encouraging warfare and thus stressing the land even more than before.

Herein lies another—and perhaps the most important—lesson worth pondering. It is no great insight to state that people's cultural biases and particularly their ideologies may blind them to important changes in the world around them. But the case of the Maya offers a potentially useful variant on this theme. The Maya leadership appears to have become increasingly isolated from the rest of society during the Late Classic period. At a time when the demands on the skills of the rulers were growing rapidly, positions of power were increasingly gained through kinship ties, not necessarily by achievement. The isolation of the elite could have made it even more difficult for them to break away from traditional modes of thought and look at critical problems from fresh vantage points. So even though the ancient Maya leadership perceived the coming crisis, they responded in a predictable, but ultimately disastrous fashion. By becoming aware of our own preconceptions and struggling to go beyond them, we may do better than the Maya.

In his insightful book *The Collapse of Complex Societies*, the archaeologist Joseph Tainter of the U.S. Forest Service has compared the collapse of civilizations from the Romans to the Puebloans of Chaco Canyon in the American Southwest. He argues that as societies become increasingly complex, a small group of elite rulers tend to benefit exclusively, and the chances of collapse grow rapidly. The Classic Maya of the Southern Lowlands fit this model very well.

Tainter points out that for over a thousand years the Maya peasantry supported upwardly spiraling numbers of monuments, agricul-

By the Terminal Classic period, metal objects were used in the Maya Lowlands, but only for ceremonial purposes. This gold frog pendant was dredged from the bottom of the Sacred Well at Chichén Itzá.

Although the jungle of the Southern Lowlands cloaks much of the glory of Classic Maya civilization, studies of Maya ecology, agriculture, and politics can not only illuminate reasons for the decline of the southern Classic Maya, but may shed light on environmental problems today.

tural projects, wars, military and civil specialists, and artisans. But a peasant's hard work did not bring a better diet; on the contrary, the health and nutrition of the population was low, and they further deteriorated during Late Classic times. With the investment in complexity bringing a lower standard of living to the majority, it is no surprise that the civilization of the southern Classic Maya eventually collapsed.

Tainter says that looked at in this light, collapses are not necessarily negative or tragic. As always, the question is, tragic for whom? In the case of Classic civilization in the Southern Lowlands, the collapse of the society was probably tragic for the elite but perhaps not for the peasants. "To a population that is receiving little return on the cost of supporting complexity, the loss of complexity brings economic . . . gains."

But does Tainter's theory fit our global society today, too? Tainter maintains that it does, although the interconnectedness of today's world makes it difficult for any one segment to collapse. Like our own world, the Maya realm was fragmented into separate political units. Tainter says, "In this sense, although industrial society . . . is sometimes likened in popular thought to ancient Rome, a close analogy would be with . . . the Maya." Tainter believes that while collapse is not imminent, given today's competitive spiral and the decreasing standard of living for many people, the possibility of total system collapse remains a strong possibility.

The question remains, how do we break this potentially disastrous spiral? Will archaeologists of the future looking at our world wonder why society took just the kinds of steps that aggravated our obvious difficulties rather than curing them? Are we locked into ways of thinking that blind us to the root causes of problems? Are we pursuing solutions that appear to make sense only because we are unable or unwilling to step back and broaden our perspective? Do we look for short-term gain at the price of long-term ruination? Do we rely too heavily on the expectation that technological innovations will bail out the system when our plight becomes critical? Are too many people missing out on the benefits of all our technological triumphs? If the answer to any of these questions is yes, then case studies like that of the Southern Lowland Maya collapse may help in a small way to open the public's eyes and those of our leaders. In the Maya example, the actions taken to solve the dire puzzles facing their civilization failed. By studying the Maya, perhaps we can learn what general kinds of efforts to avoid and how we can strengthen our chances of survival.

GENERAL INTRODUCTIONS TO THE
ANCIENT MAYA

The most complete introduction is Sylvanus Morley, George Brainerd, and Robert Sharer, *The Ancient Maya,* Fourth edition, Stanford, Stanford University Press, 1983. Other fine introductions include: Michael D. Coe, *The Maya,* Fourth edition, London and New York, Thames and Hudson, 1987; Charles Gallenkamp, *Maya,* Third revised edition, New York, Viking, 1985; Norman Hammond, *Ancient Maya Civilization,* New Brunswick, Rutgers University Press, 1982; John Henderson, *The World of the Ancient Maya,* Ithaca, Cornell University Press, 1981; and George Stuart and Gene Stuart, *The Mysterious Maya,* Washington, D.C., National Geographic Society, 1977. The best introduction to new thinking in hieroglyphic and iconographic studies is Linda Schele and Mary Ellen Miller, *The Blood of Kings,* Fort Worth, Kimbell Art Museum, 1986. George F. Andrews, *Maya Cities: Placemaking and Urbanization,* Norman, University of Oklahoma Press, 1975, and C. Gallenkamp and R. E. Johnson (editors), *Maya: Treasures of an Ancient Civilization,* New York, Harry N. Abrams, 1985, also provide fine overviews.

FURTHER

READINGS

CHAPTER ONE

BINFORD, LEWIS R., *In Pursuit of the Past.* London and New York, Thames and Hudson, 1983.

FAGAN, BRIAN, *In the Beginning: An Introduction to Archaeology,* Sixth edition. Glenview, Scott, Foresman/Little Brown College Division, 1988.

SABLOFF, JEREMY A., *The Cities of Ancient Mexico.* London and New York, Thames and Hudson, 1989.

SCHIFFER, MICHAEL B., *Formation Processes of the Archaeological Record.* Albuquerque, University of New Mexico Press, 1987.

SHARER, ROBERT J., and WENDY A. ASHMORE, *Archaeology, Discovering Our Past.* Palo Alto, Mayfield, 1987.

THOMAS, DAVID HURST, *Archaeology,* Second edition. New York, Holt, Rinehart, and Winston, 1989.

WILLEY, GORDON R., and JEREMY A. SABLOFF, *A History of American Archaeology,* Second edition. New York, W. H. Freeman, 1980.

CHAPTER TWO

BECKER, MARSHALL J., Priests, Peasants and Ceremonial Centers: The Intellectual History of a Model. In *Maya Archaeology and Ethnohistory* (edited by Norman Hammond and Gordon R. Willey), pp. 3–20. Austin, University of Texas Press, 1979.

BERNAL, IGNACIO, *A History of Mexican Archaeology.* London and New York, Thames and Hudson, 1980.

BRUNHOUSE, ROBERT L., *Sylvanus Morley and the World of the Ancient Maya.* Norman, University of Oklahoma Press, 1971.

BRUNHOUSE, ROBERT L., *In Search of the Maya.* Albuquerque, University of New Mexico Press, 1973.

BRUNHOUSE, ROBERT L., *Pursuit of the Ancient Maya.* Albuquerque, University of New Mexico Press, 1975.

EDMONSON, MUNRO S., *The Ancient Future of the Itza: The Book of Chilam Balam of Tizimin.* Austin, University of Texas Press, 1982.

GANN, THOMAS, and J. ERIC S. THOMPSON, *The History of the Maya from the Earliest Time to the Present Day.* New York, Scribner's, 1931.

HAMMOND, NORMAN, Sir Eric Thompson, 1898–1975: A Biographical Sketch and Bibliography. In *Social Process in Maya Prehistory; Studies in Honour of Sir Eric Thompson* (edited by Norman Hammond), pp. 1–18. London, Academic Press, 1977.

HAMMOND, NORMAN, Lords of the Jungle: A Prosopography of Maya Archaeology. In *Civilization in the Ancient Americas; Essays in Honor of Gordon R. Willey* (edited by Richard M. Leventhal and Alan L. Kolata), pp. 3–32. Albuquerque, University of New Mexico Press and the Peabody Museum, Harvard University, 1983.

JOYCE, THOMAS A., *Mexican Archaeology.* New York, G. P. Putnam's Sons, 1914.

KLUCKHOHN, CLYDE, The Conceptual Structure in Middle American Archaeology. In *The Maya and their Neighbors* (edited by C. L. Hay et al.), pp. 41–51. New York, D. Appleton-Century, 1940.

MATTHEWSON, KENT, Maya Urban Genesis Reconsidered: Trade and Intensive Agriculture as Primary Factors. *Journal of Historical Geography,* Vol. 3, No. 3, pp. 203–215, 1977.

MAUDSLAY, ALFRED P. *Archaeology (Biologia Centrali Americana,* 4 vols. plates, 1 vol. text). London, Taylor and Francis, 1889–1902.

MERWIN, R. E., and GEORGE C. VAILLANT, *The Ruins of Holmul, Guatemala.* Memoirs of the Peabody Museum, Harvard University, Vol. 3, No. 2, 1932.

MORLEY, SYLVANUS G., *The Ancient Maya*. Stanford, Stanford University Press, 1946 (later editions in 1947, 1956, and 1983).

POLLOCK, HARRY E. D. Sources and Methods in the Study of Maya Architecture. In *The Maya and Their Neighbors* (edited by C. L. Hay et al.), pp. 179–201. New York, D. Appleton-Century, 1940.

POLLOCK, HARRY E. D., *The Puuc: An Archaeological Survey of the Hill Country of Yucatan and Northern Campeche, Mexico*. Memoirs of the Peabody Museum, Harvard University, Vol. 19, 1980.

POLLOCK, HARRY E. D., RALPH L. ROYS, TATIANA PROSKOURIAKOFF, and A. LEDYARD SMITH, *Mayapan, Yucatan, Mexico*. Carnegie Institution of Washington Publication 619, 1962.

PROSKOURIAKOFF, TATIANA, *An Album of Maya Architecture*. Carnegie Institution of Washington Publication 558, 1946 (reprinted in 1963 by the University of Oklahoma Press).

RICKETSON, OLIVER G., and EDITH B. RICKETSON, *Uaxactún, Guatemala, Group E, 1926–1937*. Carnegie Institution of Washington Publication 477, 1937.

SABLOFF, JEREMY A., PATRICIA A. MCANANY, BERND FAHMEL BEYER, TOMÁS GALLARETA NEGRON, SIGNA L. LARRALDE, and LUANN WANDSNIDER, *Ancient Maya Settlement Patterns at the Site of Sayil, Puuc Region, Yucatan, Mexico: Initial Reconnaissance (1983)*. Latin American Institute, University of New Mexico, Research Paper Series No. 14, 1984.

SMITH, A. LEDYARD, *Uaxactún, Guatemala: Excavations of 1931–1937*. Carnegie Institution of Washington Publication 588, 1950.

SMITH, A. LEDYARD, *Uaxactún: A Pioneering Excavation in Guatemala*. Addison–Wesley Module in Anthropology, No. 40, 1973.

SMITH, ROBERT E., *Ceramic Sequence at Uaxactún, Guatemala*, 2 vols. Middle American Research Institute, Tulane University, Publication 20, 1955.

SPINDEN, HERBERT J., *A Study of Maya Art*. Memoirs of the Peabody Museum, Harvard University, Vol. 6, 1913.

STEPHENS, JOHN L., *Incidents of Travel in Central America, Chiapas and Yucatán*, 2 vols. New York, Harper, 1841 (reprinted in 1962 by Dover).

STEPHENS, JOHN L., *Incidents of Travel in Yucatán*, 2 vols. New York, Harper, 1843 (reprinted in 1963 by Dover).

THOMPSON, J. ERIC S., *The Civilization of the Mayas*. Field Museum of Natural History, Leaflet 25, 1927 (plus many later editions).

THOMPSON, J. ERIC S., *The Rise and Fall of Maya Civilization*. Norman, University of Oklahoma Press, 1954 (later edition in 1966).

THOMPSON, J. ERIC S., *Maya Archaeologist*. Norman, University of Oklahoma Press, 1963.

TOURTELLOT, GAIR, JEREMY A. SABLOFF, PATRICIA A. MCANANY, THOMAS W. KILLION, KELLI CARMEAN, RAFAEL COBOS PALMA, CHRISTOPHER DORE, BERND FAHMEL BEYER, SANDRA LOPEZ VARELA, CARLOS PEREZ ALVAREZ, and SUSAN WURTZBURG, *Archaeological Investigations at Sayil, Yucatán, Mexico, Phase II: The 1987 Field Season*. University of Pittsburgh Anthropological Papers No. 1, 1989.

TOZZER, ALFRED M., *A Comparative Study of the Mayas and Lacandons*. Archaeological Institute of America, New York, Macmillan, 1907.

TOZZER, ALFRED M., (editor), *Landa's Relacion de las cosas de Yucatán*. Papers of the Peabody Museum, Harvard University, Vol. 28, 1941.

CHAPTER THREE

ADAMS, RICHARD E. W., *The Ceramics of Altar de Sacrificios*. Papers of the Peabody Museum, Harvard University, Vol. 63, No. 1, 1971.

ADAMS, RICHARD E. W., W. E. BROWN, JR., and T. PATRICK CULBERT, Radar Mapping, Archaeology, and Ancient Maya Land Use. *Science*, Vol. 213, No. 4515, pp. 1457–1463, 1981.

BECKER, MARSHALL J., Archaeological Evidence for Occupational Specialization Among the Classic Period Maya at Tikal, Guatemala. *American Antiquity*, Vol. 38, pp. 396–406, 1973.

CHASE, ARLEN F., and DIANE Z. CHASE, The Investigation of Classic Period Maya Warfare at Caracol, Belize. *Mayab*, No. 5, pp. 5–18, 1989.

COE, WILLIAM R., Tikal: Ten Years of Study of a Maya Ruin in the Lowlands of Guatemala. *Expedition*, Vol. 8, No. 1, pp. 5–56, 1965.

COE, WILLIAM R., *Tikal: A Handbook of the Ancient Maya Ruins*. Philadelphia, University Museum, 1967.

COGGINS, CLEMENCY, A New Order and the Role of the Calendar: Some Characteristics of the Middle Classic Period at Tikal. In *Maya Archaeology and Ethnohistory* (edited by Norman Hammond and Gordon R. Willey), pp. 38–50. Austin, University of Texas Press, 1979.

FLANNERY, KENT V. (editor), *Maya Subsistence: Studies in Memory of Dennis E. Puleston*. New York, Academic Press, 1982.

GANN, THOMAS, and J. ERIC S. THOMPSON, *The History of the Maya from the Earliest Time to the Present Day*. New York, Scribner's, 1931.

HAMBLIN, NANCY L., *Animal Use by the Cozumel Maya*. Tucson, University of Arizona Press, 1984.

HARRISON, PETER D., and B. L. TURNER (editors), *Pre-Hispanic Maya Agriculture*. Albuquerque, University of New Mexico Press, 1978.

HAVILAND, WILLIAM A., Prehistoric Settlement at Tikal, Guatemala. *Expedition*, Vol. 7, No. 3, pp. 15–23, 1965.

HOUSTON, STEPHEN D., The Phonetic Decipherment of Mayan Glyphs. *Antiquity*, Vol. 62, No. 234, pp. 126–135, 1988.

HOUSTON, STEPHEN D., Archaeology and Maya Writing. *Journal of World Prehistory*, Vol. 3, No. 1, pp. 1–32, 1989.

JONES, CHRISTOPHER, WILLIAM R. COE, and WILLIAM A. HAVILAND, Tikal: An Outline of Its Field Study (1956–1970) and a Project Bibliography. In *Supplement to the Handbook of Middle American Indians*, Vol. 1: Archaeology (Victoria R. Bricker, General Editor and Jeremy A. Sabloff, Volume Editor), pp. 296–312. Austin, University of Texas Press, 1981.

KILLION, THOMAS W., JEREMY A. SABLOFF, GAIR TOURTELLOT, and NICHOLAS P. DUNNING, Intensive Surface Collection of Residential Clusters at Terminal Classic Sayil (A.D. 800–1000), Yucatán, Mexico. *Journal of Field Archaeology*, Vol. 16, 1989.

MARCUS, JOYCE, The Iconography of Power Among the Classic Maya. *World Archaeology*, Vol. 6, pp. 83–94, 1974.

MARCUS, JOYCE, *Emblem and State in the Classic Maya Lowlands*. Washington, D.C., Dumbarton Oaks, 1976.

MCANANY, PATRICIA A., Stone-Tool Production and Exchange in the Eastern Maya Lowlands: The Consumer Perspective from Pulltrouser Swamp, Belize. *American Antiquity*, Vol. 54, No. 2, pp. 332–346, 1989.

MILLER, ARTHUR G., *Maya Rulers of Time*. Philadelphia, University Museum, 1986.

POLLOCK, HARRY E. D., Architecture of the Maya Lowlands. In *Handbook of Middle American Indians*, Vol. 2 (Robert Wauchope, General Editor, and Gordon R. Willey, Volume Editor), pp. 378–440. Austin, University of Texas Press, 1965.

PROSKOURIAKOFF, TATIANA, Lords of the Maya Realm. *Expedition*, Vol. 4, No. 1, pp. 14–21, 1961.

RATHJE, WILLIAM L., Socio-Political Implications of Lowland Maya

Burials: Methodology and Tentative Hypotheses. *World Archaeology*, Vol. 1, pp. 359–374, 1970.

RICE, DON S., and PRUDENCE M. RICE, Lessons from the Maya. *Latin American Research Review*, Vol. 19, No. 3, pp. 7–34, 1984.

RUE, DAVID J., Early Agriculture and Early Postclassic Maya Occupation in Western Honduras. *Nature*, Vol. 326, No. 6110, pp. 285–286, 1987.

SABLOFF, JEREMY A. (editor), *Analyses of Fine Paste Ceramics.* Memoirs of the Peabody Museum, Harvard University, Vol. 15, No. 2, 1982.

SABLOFF, JEREMY A., and GAIR TOURTELLOT, *The Ancient Maya City of Sayil: The Mapping of a Puuc Region Center* (in press).

SABLOFF, JEREMY A., and GORDON R. WILLEY, The Collapse of Maya Civilization in the Southern Lowlands: A Consideration of History and Process. *Southwestern Journal of Anthropology*, Vol. 23, pp. 311–336, 1967.

SANDERS, WILLIAM T., and BARBARA J. PRICE, *Mesoamerica: The Evolution of a Civilization.* New York, Random House, 1968.

SIEMENS, ALFRED H., and DENNIS E. PULESTON, Ridged Fields and Associated Features in Southern Campeche: New Perspectives on the Lowland Maya. *American Antiquity*, Vol. 37, pp. 228–239, 1972.

TAYLOR, WALTER W., *A Study of Archaeology.* Memoirs of the American Anthropological Association, No. 69, 1948 (reprinted in 1967 by the Southern Illinois University Press).

THOMPSON, J. ERIC S., *Maya Hieroglyphic Writing: An Introduction.* Carnegie Institution of Washington Publication 589, 1950 (Third edition published in 1971 by the University of Oklahoma Press).

TURNER, B. L., II, and PETER D. HARRISON (editors), *Pulltrouser Swamp: Ancient Maya Habitat, Agriculture, and Settlement in Northern Belize.* Austin, University of Oklahoma Press, 1983.

WEBSTER, DAVID L., *Defensive Earthworks at Becan, Campeche, Mexico.* Middle American Research Institute, Tulane University, Publication 41, 1976.

WEBSTER, DAVID L., Warfare and the Evolution of Maya Civilization. In *The Origins of Maya Civilization* (edited by R. E. W. Adams), pp. 335–372. Albuquerque, University of New Mexico Press, 1977.

WILLEY, GORDON R., *Prehistoric Settlement Patterns in the Viru Valley, Peru.* Bureau of American Ethnology, Bulletin 155, 1953.

WILLEY, GORDON R., *Portraits in American Archaeology: Remembrances of Some Distinguished Americanists.* Albuquerque, University of New Mexico Press, 1988.

WILLEY, GORDON R., WILLIAM R. BULLARD, JR., JOHN B. GLASS, and JAMES C. GIFFORD, *Prehistoric Maya Settlements in the Belize Valley.* Papers of the Peabody Museum, Harvard University, Vol. 54, 1965.

CHAPTER FOUR

ADAMS, RICHARD E. W. (editor), *The Origins of Maya Civilization.* Albuquerque, University of New Mexico Press, 1977.

ANDREWS, ANTHONY P., TOMÁS GALLARETA NEGRON, FERNANDO ROBLES CASTELLANOS, RAFAEL COBOS PALMA, and PURA CERVERA RIVERO, Isla Cerritos, An Itzá Trading Port on the North Coast of Yucatán, Mexico. *National Geographic Research,* Vol. 4, No. 2, pp. 196–207, 1988.

ANDREWS, E. WYLLYS, IV, and E. WYLLYS ANDREWS V, *Excavations at Dzibilchaltún, Yucatán, Mexico.* Middle American Research Institute, Tulane University, Publication 48, 1980.

ANDREWS, E. WYLLYS, V, The Early Ceramic History of the Lowland Maya. In *Vision and Revision in Maya Studies* (edited by Peter D. Harrison and Flora Clancy). Albuquerque, University of New Mexico Press (in press).

ANDREWS, E. WYLLYS, V, WILLIAM M. RINGLE III, PHILIP J. BARNES, ALFREDO BARRERA RUBIO, and TOMÁS GALLARETA NEGRON, Komchén: An Early Maya Community in Northwest Yucatán. In *Investigaciones recientes en el area Maya,* Vol. 1, pp. 73–92. XVII Mesa Redonda, Mexico, D.F., Sociedad Mexicana de Antropología, 1984.

CHASE, ARLEN F., and PRUDENCE M. RICE (editors), *The Lowland Maya Postclassic.* Austin, University of Texas Press, 1985.

CULBERT, T. PATRICK, *The Classic Maya Collapse.* Albuquerque, University of New Mexico Press, 1973.

FREIDEL, DAVID A., and JEREMY A. SABLOFF, *Cozumel: Late Maya Settlement Patterns.* New York, Academic Press, 1984.

HAMMOND, NORMAN, The Earliest Maya. *Scientific American,* Vol. 236, No. 3, pp. 116–133, 1977.

HOSLER, DOROTHY, JEREMY A. SABLOFF, and DALE RUNGE, Simulation Model Development: A Case Study of the Classic Maya Collapse. In *Social Process in Maya Prehistory; Studies in Honour of Sir Eric Thompson* (edited by Norman Hammond), pp. 553–590. London, Academic Press, 1977.

MATHENY, RAY T., Investigations at El Mirador, Peten, Guatemala. *National Geographic Research*, Vol. 2, pp. 332–353, 1986.

PENDERGAST, DAVID M., Lamanai, Belize: Summary of Excavation Results, 1974–1980. *Journal of Field Archaeology*, Vol. 8, No. 1, pp. 29–53, 1981.

RATHJE, WILLIAM L., The Last Tango in Mayapán: A Tentative Trajectory of Production-Distribution Systems. In *Ancient Civilization and Trade* (edited by Jeremy A. Sabloff and C. C. Lamberg-Karlovsky), pp. 409–448. Albuquerque, University of New Mexico Press, 1975.

ROBERTSON, ROBIN A., and DAVID A. FREIDEL (editors), *Archaeology at Cerros, Belize, Central America*, Volume I: An Interim Report. Dallas, Southern Methodist University Press, 1986.

SABLOFF, JEREMY A., Old Myths, New Myths: The Role of Sea Traders in the Development of Ancient Maya Civilization. In *The Sea in the Pre-Columbian World* (edited by E. Benson), pp. 67–88. Washington, D.C., Dumbarton Oaks, 1977.

SABLOFF, JEREMY A., and E. WYLLYS ANDREWS V (editors), *Late Lowland Maya Civilization: Classic to Postclassic*. Albuquerque, University of New Mexico Press, 1986.

SABLOFF, JEREMY A., and WILLIAM L. RATHJE (editors), *A Study of Changing Precolumbian Commercial Systems*, Monographs of the Peabody Museum, Harvard University, No. 3, 1975.

SHEETS, PAYSON D., Maya Recovery from Volcanic Disasters, Ilopango and Ceren. *Archaeology*, Vol. 32, No. 3, pp. 32–42, 1979.

CHAPTER FIVE

ANDREWS, ANTHONY P., TOMÁS GALLARETA NEGRON, FERNANDO ROBLES CASTELLANOS, RAFAEL COBOS PALMA, and PURA CERVERA RIVERO, Isla Cerritos, an Itzá Trading Port on the North Coast of Yucatán, Mexico. *National Geographic Research*, Vol. 4, No. 2, pp. 196–207, 1988.

ANDREWS, ANTHONY P., FRANK ASARO, HELEN V. MICHEL, F. H. STROSS, and PURA CERVERA RIVERO, The Obsidian Trade at Isla Cerritos, Yucatán, Mexico. *Journal of Field Archaeology*, Vol. 16, 1989.

ASHMORE, WENDY (editor), *Lowland Maya Settlement Patterns*. Albuquerque, University of New Mexico Press, 1981.

CULBERT, T. PATRICK, Political History and the Decipherment of Maya Glyphs. *Antiquity*, Vol. 62, No. 234, pp. 135–152, 1988.

FASH, WILLIAM L., JR., A New Look at Maya Statecraft from Copán, Honduras. *Antiquity*, Vol. 62, No. 234, pp. 157–169, 1988.

MARCUS, JOYCE, Lowland Maya Archaeology at the Crossroads. *American Antiquity*, Vol. 48, No. 3, pp. 454–488, 1983.

MARCUS, JOYCE, On the Nature of the Mesoamerican City. In *Prehistoric Settlement Patterns: Essays in Honor of Gordon R. Willey* (edited by Evon Z. Vogt and Richard M. Leventhal), pp. 195–242. Albuquerque, University of New Mexico Press and Peabody Museum, Harvard University, 1983.

MILLER, MARY ELLEN, *The Art of Mesoamerica: From Olmec to Aztec*. London and New York, Thames and Hudson, 1986.

PROSKOURIAKOFF, TATIANA, *Jades from the Cenote of Sacrifice, Chichén Itzá, Yucatán*. Memoirs of the Peabody Museum, Harvard University, Vol. 10, No. 1. Cambridge, 1974.

RICE, PRUDENCE M., Economic Change in the Lowland Maya Late Classic Period. In *Specialization, Exchange, and Complex Societies* (edited by Elizabeth M. Brumfiel and Timothy K. Earle), pp. 76–85. Cambridge, Cambridge University Press, 1987.

SABLOFF, JEREMY A., Ancient Maya Civilization. In *Maya: Treasures of an Ancient Civilization* (edited by Charles Gallenkamp and Regina Elise Johnson), pp. 34–46. New York, Harry N. Abrams, 1985.

SABLOFF, JEREMY A., PATRICIA A. MCANANY, BERND FAHMEL BEYER, TOMÁS GALLARETA NEGRON, SIGNA L. LARRALDE, and LUANN WANDSNIDER, *Ancient Maya Settlement Patterns at the Site of Sayil, Puuc Region, Yucatán, Mexico: Initial Reconnaissance (1983)*. Latin American Institute, University of New Mexico, Research Paper Series No. 14, 1984.

TOURTELLOT, GAIR, JEREMY A. SABLOFF, PATRICIA A. MCANANY, THOMAS W. KILLION, KELLI CARMEAN, RAFAEL COBOS PALMA, CHRISTOPHER DORE, BERND FAHMEL BEYER, SANDRA LOPEZ VARELA, CARLOS PEREZ ALVAREZ, and SUSAN WURTZBURG, *Archaeological Investigations at Sayil, Yucatán, Mexico, Phase II: The 1987 Field Season*. University of Pittsburgh Anthropological Papers No. 1, 1989.

WEBSTER, DAVID L., and NANCY GONLIN, Household Remains of the Humblest Maya. *Journal of Field Archaeology*, Vol. 15, pp. 169–190, 1988.

WILLEY, GORDON R., *Essays in Maya Archaeology*. Albuquerque, University of New Mexico Press, 1987.

CHAPTER SIX

BECKER, MARSHALL J., Priests, Peasants and Ceremonial Centers: The Intellectual History of a Model. In *Maya Archaeology and Ethnohistory* (edited by Norman Hammond and Gordon R. Willey), pp. 3–20. Austin, University of Texas Press, 1979.

FORD, RICHARD I., Archaeology Serving Humanity. In *Research and Theory in Current Archaeology* (edited by Charles L. Redman), pp. 83–93. New York, Wiley-Interscience, 1973.

HODDER, IAN, *Reading the Past: Current Approaches to Interpretation in Archaeology.* Cambridge, Cambridge University Press, 1986.

MATTHEWSON, KENT, Maya Urban Genesis Reconsidered: Trade and Intensive Agriculture as Primary Factors. *Journal of Historical Geography*, Vol. 3, No. 3, pp. 203–215, 1977.

RICE, DON S., and PRUDENCE M. RICE, Lessons from the Maya. *Latin American Research Review*, Vol. 19, No. 3, pp. 7–34, 1984.

SABLOFF, JEREMY A., The Collapse of Classic Maya Civilization. In *The Patient Earth* (edited by John Harte and Robert H. Socolow), pp. 16–27. New York, Holt, Rinehart and Winston, 1971.

TAINTER, JOSEPH A., *The Collapse of Complex Societies.* Cambridge, Cambridge University Press, 1988.

WILK, RICHARD R., The Ancient Maya and the Political Present. *Journal of Anthropological Research*, Vol. 41, No. 3, pp. 307–326, 1985.

SOURCES

OF

ILLUSTRATIONS

PAGE 37
Peabody Museum, Harvard
University

PAGE 38
Diego Molina

PAGE 42
Peabody Museum, Harvard
University. Photograph by Carnegie
Institution of Washington. Photo no.
CIW Uax 44–II–32.

PAGE 44
Peabody Museum, Harvard
University. Ink and wash by Tatiana
Proskouriakoff. Photo no. T935.

PAGE 46
Peabody Museum, Harvard
University. Drawings by Tatiana
Proskouriakoff. Photo no. N27675
and N27679.

PAGE 48
Courtesy of the author

PAGE 51
From *Book of Chilam Balam of
Chumayel*, Latin American Collection,
Princeton University Library.
Courtesy of Munro Edmonson.

PAGE 52
From J. Eric S. Thompson, *Maya
Archaeologist*. Norman, University of
Oklahoma Press, 1963.

PAGE 53
Donald Thompson

PAGE 55
The Museum of New Mexico. Photo
by Jesse Nusbaum. Negative no.
60861.

PAGE 58
Peabody Museum, Harvard
University

PAGE 59
Courtesy of the author

PAGE 60
Courtesy of the author

PAGE 61
Courtesy of the author

PAGE 63
Adapted from Doris Heyden and
Paul Gendorp, *Pre–Columbian
Architecture of Mesoamerica*.

PAGES 66 AND 67
Peabody Museum, Harvard
University. Copy of fresco by
Antonio Tejeda. Photo no. T 1051 F.

PAGE 69
Gordon Willey

PAGE 71
Gordon Willey

PAGE 72
Courtesy of the author

PAGE 73
Courtesy of the author

PAGE 74
Courtesy of the author

PAGE 76
Peter Harrison

PAGE 77
The University Museum, University
of Pennsylvania, Tikal Project

PAGE 79
Museo Nacional de Arqueología y
Etnología, Guatemala. Photograph
by Stuart Rome. Courtesy of the
Albuquerque Museum.

PAGE 80
The University Museum, University
of Pennsylvania

PAGE 82
B. L. Turner II

PAGE 83
Peter Harrison

PAGE 84
From R. E. W. Adams, W. E.
Brown, Jr., and T. Patrick Culbert,
"Radar Mapping, Archaeology, and
Ancient Maya Land Use." *Science*,
Vol. 213, p. 1460, AAAS, 25
September 1981.

PAGE 85
Peabody Museum, Harvard
University. Copy of fresco by
Antonio Tejeda. Photo no. T 1051 F.

PAGE 86
Merle Greene Robertson

PAGE 87
© National Geographic Society

PAGE 88
Adapted from David Webster,
*Defensive Earthworks at Becan,
Campeche, Mexico*, Publication 41,
Figure 104. Middle American
Research Institute, Tulane
University, 1976.

PAGE 90
Courtesy of the author

PAGE 91
Courtesy of the author

PAGE 93
left, Merle Greene Robertson

PAGE 94
The University Museum, University
of Pennsylvania

PAGE 95
Redrawn from William A. Haviland,
Anthropology, Fifth Edition. New York,
Holt, Rinehart, and Winston, 1989.

PAGE 97
Redrawn from *The Ancient Maya,*
Fourth Edition, by Sylvanus G.
Morley and George W. Brainerd,
revised by Robert J. Sharer; with the
permission of the publishers,
Stanford University Press, © 1946,
1947, 1956, 1983, by the Board of
Trustees of the Leland Stanford
Junior University.

PAGE 98
Adapted from Gordon Willey,
Excavations at Seibal: Artifacts.

PAGE 99
© National Geographic Society

PAGE 101
left, Macduff Everton
right, Museo Regional de
Antropología, Merida. Photograph
by Stuart Rome. Courtesy of the
Albuquerque Museum.

PAGE 102
The University Museum, University
of Pennsylvania

PAGE 103
Middle American Research Institute

PAGE 104
Museo Nacional de Arqueología y
Etnología, Guatemala. Photograph
by Stuart Rome. Courtesy of the
Albuquerque Museum.

PAGE 105
Courtesy of the author

PAGE 106
Thomas R. Hester, Colha Project

PAGE 108
Merle Greene Robertson

PAGES 110 AND 111
Macduff Everton

PAGE 113
Middle American Research Institute

PAGE 114
top, The University Museum,
University of Pennsylvania
bottom, Gordon Willey

PAGE 116
David Freidel

PAGE 117
Adapted from a drawing by Stanley
Loten. Courtesy of David
Pendergast.

PAGE 119
Ermgard Groth, courtesy of Merle
Green Robertson

PAGE 120
Frank Saul

PAGE 121
Adapted from Dorothy Hosler,
Jeremy Sabloff, and Dale Runge,
"Simulation Model Development: A
Case Study of the Maya Collapse"
in *Social Process in Maya Prehistory,*
edited by N. Hammond

PAGE 123
Macduff Everton

PAGE 124
top, Macduff Everton
bottom, courtesy of the author

PAGE 125
Peter Harrison

PAGE 126
top, Middle American Research
Institute
bottom, Peter Harrison

PAGE 127
Macduff Everton

PAGE 128
Merle Greene Robertson

PAGE 129
Ermgard Groth, courtesy of Merle
Greene Robertson

PAGE 131
Peabody Museum, Harvard
University

PAGE 132
Middle American Research Institute

PAGE 133
Courtesy of the author

PAGES 136 AND 137
Otis Imboden, courtesy of Museo
Nacional de Arqueología y
Etnología, Guatemala. © National
Geographic Society.

PAGE 138
Merle Greene Robertson

PAGE 139
Museo Nacional de Arqueología y
Etnología, Guatemala. Photograph
by Stuart Rome. Courtesy of the
Albuquerque Museum.

PAGE 141
left, Peabody Museum, Harvard
University. Photograph by Hillel
Burger. Photo no. 10–71–20/C6674.
right, David Pendergast

PAGE 142
Ian Graham

PAGE 143
Merle Greene Robertson

PAGE 144
Merle Greene Robertson

PAGE 146
Macduff Everton

PAGE 147
Peter Harrison

PAGE 148
Macduff Everton

PAGE 150
Museo Regional de Antropología, Merida. Photograph by Stuart Rome. Courtesy of the Albuquerque Museum.

PAGE 153
Middle American Research Institute

PAGE 154
Courtesy of the author

PAGE 155
Courtesy of the author

PAGE 156
Anthony Andrews

PAGE 157
Adapted from Anthony Andrews, et al., "Isla Cerritos: An Itzá Trading Port on the North Coast of Yucatán, Mexico," Figure 1. *National Geographic Research*, Vol. 4, No. 2, 1988.

PAGE 158
C. Rasmunsen, courtesy of Anthony Andrews

PAGE 159
Courtesy of the author

PAGE 160
George Stuart

PAGE 162
David Webster

PAGES 164 AND 165
Macduff Everton

PAGE 167
Adapted from Richard Wilk, "The Ancient Maya and the Political Present," Figure 1. *Journal of Anthropological Research*, Vol. 41, No. 3, 1985.

PAGE 168
The University Museum, University of Pennsylvania

PAGE 170
Peter Harrison

PAGE 171
Frans Lanting

PAGE 172
William Garnett

PAGE 173
Peabody Museum, Harvard University. Photograph by Hillel Burger. Photo no. T812.

PAGE 174
Macduff Everton

INDEX

Other books in the Scientific American Library Series